A Pilgrim's Guide *to*

THE
SPIRIT
FILLED
LIFE

A Pilgrim's Guide *to*

THE
SPIRIT
FILLED
LIFE

Rediscovering *the* Gift *of the* Spirit

Sean Azzaro

302 BOOKS

2301 Lucien Way #415
Maitland, FL 32751
407.339.4217
www.302books.com

302
BOOKS

A Pilgrim's Guide to the Spirit-Filled Life:
Rediscovering the Gift of the Spirit

Printed in the United States of America.
ISBN-13: 978-1-6305-0188-4
Library of Congress Number: 2020900675

DEDICATION

To my beautiful wife, Lauri, whose love, encouragement, and partnership have been the better half of our life and work together all these years.

To the Holy Spirit, Who really is the friend who sticks closer than a brother and Who resides in every follower of Jesus.

Acknowledgments

Special thanks to...

Dr. Larry Keefauver for your guidance, effort, and editing of this book.

My wife, Lauri, for reading, proofing, and giving perspective on every word of this book.

Kristy Rivers (one very cool assistant), for working on transcripts, fighting with schedules, and basically doing whatever it took to get this done.

Agatha Kerr, for editing the manuscript.

Amy Wren, for proofreading the manuscript.

The people of River City Community Church for showing me what the Spirit-filled life could look like in biblical community!

TABLE OF CONTENTS

Foreword by Melanie Shankle xi

Introduction xiii

Part One: The Spirit-Filled Life 1

Insight 1: Something Real 3

Insight 2: Missing the Point. 8

Insight 3: Learning to Fly. 13

Insight 4: Becoming Like Him 17

Insight 5: Filled with Love 21

Insight 6: Wisdom and Understanding. 25

Insight 7: Never Thirst Again. 29

Insight 8: Being Filled 34

Part Two: A New Life 39

Insight 9: False Advertising. 41

Insight 10: Three Laws. 46

Insight 11: The Nature of Fruit 50

Insight 12: The Hope of Holiness 54

Insight 13: Wind Power versus Willpower. 58

Insight 14: Learning to Hear 62

Part Three: Spirit-Filled Prayer 67

Insight 15: The Power to Change the World 69

Insight 16: Always Praying. 74

Insight 17: Praying in the Spirit. 79

Insight 18: Praying the Mind of Christ 84

Insight 19: Your Prayer Partner. 88

Part Four: Spirit-Filled Worship. **93**
    Insight 20: Spiritual Communion 95
    Insight 21: The Truth of Worship 99
    Insight 22: The Spirit of Worship 103
    Insight 23: Heart to Heart. 107
    Insight 24: Living Sacrifice. 111
    Insight 25: Alignment with the Throne 115

Part Five: Spirit-Filled Power. **121**
    Insight 26: The Power of the Spirit. 123
    Insight 27: Talk is Cheap 128
    Insight 28: Are You Crazy?. 132
    Insight 29: Natural versus Spiritual Gifts 136
    Insight 30: No Exceptions 141

Part Six: Spirit-Filled Speech **145**
    Insight 31: Let the Spirit Speak. 147
    Insight 32: Spiritual Language. 151
    Insight 33: Why Tongues?. 156
    Insight 34: The Gift of Prophecy. 160
    Insight 35: The Boldness to Speak 164
    Insight 36: One More Thing 168

Experience the Spirit-Filled Life: Action Steps **173**
Notes. **209**
About the Author. **211**

FOREWORD

"SEAN AZZARO HAS BEEN MY PASTOR FOR MOST OF my adult life and, so here's what I know for sure, he lives what he preaches. In a world full of people who want to tell us how we should live, Sean is a real example of what it means to actually live a life walking in the truth of God's Word. The fruit of his commitment to that principle is evident in all aspects of his life.

In his new book, *A Pilgrim's Guide to the Spirit-Filled Life*, Sean lays out exactly what that means for each of us and all the things Jesus promised us could be ours through His Spirit; wisdom, joy, contentment, discipline, and peace. You'll find that each daily reading is practical, applicable, and encouraging, no matter where you are in your faith journey. Sean has the ability to speak to the very heart of what matters most in a real and attainable way.

I found myself both challenged and encouraged by his words and the practical applications on how to consciously make God's Spirit a reality in my daily life. You will turn the last pages of *A Pilgrim's Guide* with a better understanding of what the Spirit-filled life truly means and how it relates to the abundant life that God offers every single one of us."

-Melanie Shankle,
New York Times best-selling author and speaker

INTRODUCTION

Why a book called *A Pilgrim's Guide to the Spirit-Filled Life*?

A SIMPLE ANSWER MIGHT BE, "BECAUSE THAT'S the journey, or pilgrimage, I've been on for most of my life." I grew up attending a Pentecostal church on the outskirts of Chicago, Illinois. The kind of church where good preachin' (sorry, including the "g" would completely ruin the phrase) got louder and more southern as the sermon progressed. This is particularly striking when you recall we were a suburb of Chicago. In spite of some of the cultural quirks, my family and I were blessed to be part of a wonderful church that taught us the importance of loving God and loving others. It certainly wasn't perfect, but that church displayed a passion for the Lord's presence and a true concern for people that was contagious. When I hear the horror stories that some people tell of their church upbringing, I cringe for them, but I also whisper a prayer of gratitude for my early experience in Christian community.

Of course, our church and others like it also taught, emphasized, and even identified ourselves by the present, active, and full ministry of the Holy Spirit as described and experienced in the New Testament. This included all the gifts, all the miracles, and the full ministry of the Spirit seen in the book of Acts and the Epistles. This was a significant doctrinal distinction and I learned that we were "Full Gospel," implying that those who taught differently when it came to the Spirit were partial Gospel, or something like that. However, as I grew older, I began to notice some excesses and imbalances in parts of our movement, and even in our own fellowship, when it came to things of the Spirit. As I studied more deeply, it seemed like many of our interpretations and applications went beyond what was taught and modeled in the New Testament. It felt like we gave certain manifestations and practices greater emphasis than the Scriptures did.

I vividly remember attending a series of meetings at one of our churches where a teacher taught for five consecutive nights on 1 Corinthians 14:5; "Now I want you all to speak in tongues..." He was strongly declaring that every person must speak in tongues to fully realize God's intended plan for them, almost to the point of attaching it to our salvation. Sadly, while I felt like this grossly misrepresented the Scripture's teaching, what bothered me most was the way he taught the passage.

In five nights, he never finished the verse. Seriously, he would quote the first phrase and never finish the verse! Here is what the passage actually says:

> Now I want you all to speak in tongues, but even more to prophesy. The one who prophesies is greater than the one who speaks in tongues, unless someone interprets, so that the church may be built up (1 Corinthians 14:5).

To those in attendance, the fact that the verse obviously says something very different than what was being presented didn't seem to matter, because it reinforced some of our cherished doctrines. If this was just one instance of abuse, it would simply be a cautionary tale. But sadly, it wasn't. Throughout the years this kind of imbalance and distortion has led many people and churches to not only reject flawed interpretations, **but to subtly marginalize the gift and the work of the Holy Spirit altogether.**

And that is the real reason for this book.

Throughout my thirty-plus years of pastoral ministry, which has now included churches inside and outside of Pentecostal or Charismatic circles, I have observed countless people who, in reaction to error, have shied away from what the Scriptures teach about the Holy Spirit. Consequently, they have missed out on many of the blessings that accompany God's greatest gift— His presence within us. This is a tragic example of throwing out the baby with the bathwater.

Consider this startling statement from Jesus: "Nevertheless, I tell you the truth: it is to your advantage that I go away, for if I do not go away, the Helper will not come to you. But if I go, I will send him to you" (John 16:7).

Stop and chew on that for a moment.

As incredible as the physical presence of Jesus was, there was something better and more advantageous yet to come— the Holy Spirit, Who would live in each of us every day. The Bible paints a vivid picture of the life-changing, eternity-shaping, world-altering impact of God's Spirit living and moving in us.

This book is an attempt to explore the Spirit-filled life as presented in scripture.

Let me state right up front: This is not some doctrinal defense or debate... far from it. This book is simply intended to examine and unpack various scriptures that speak to the ministry of the Holy Spirit in the life of the believer. It is actually organized into a devotional format with manageable, daily readings. Each day begins with a scripture and ends with a prayer. My hope is that you will examine the Scriptures with fresh eyes, be challenged and stimulated by some of my observations and questions, and then just take some time to let the Lord speak to you about the role of His Spirit in your life.

The goal of this book is to simply make you hungry for more of the Spirit.

At the end of the book, I have compiled a month's worth of brief, daily reminders and practical applications for you to continually practice what you discover. The end game is not just greater knowledge, but rather that you and I would continually grow in our experience of the Spirit-filled life.

Let the journey begin.

PART ONE: THE SPIRIT-FILLED LIFE

"I believe firmly, that the moment our hearts are emptied of pride and selfishness and ambition and self-seeking, and everything that is contrary to God's law, the Holy Ghost will come and fill every corner of our hearts; but if we are full of pride and conceit, and ambition and self-seeking, and pleasure and the world, there is no room for the Spirit of God; and I believe many a man is praying to God to fill him when he is full already with something else. Before we pray that God would fill us, I believe we ought to pray Him to empty us."

-Dwight L Moody [1]

Therefore, do not be unwise, but understand what the will of the Lord is. And do not be drunk with wine, in which is dissipation; but be filled with the Spirit, speaking to one another in psalms and hymns and spiritual songs, singing and making melody in your heart to the Lord, giving thanks always for all things to God the Father in the name of our Lord Jesus Christ, submitting to one another in the fear of God.

(Ephesians 5:17-21 NKJV)

Insight
-1-

SOMETHING REAL

"Truly, truly, I say to you, unless one is born of water and the
Spirit, he cannot enter the kingdom of God."
- Jesus in John 3:5

NICODEMUS WASN'T SURE WHAT TO DO. AS A leader in a very predictable and regimented religious sect, he was accustomed to having and giving the answers. Truth be told, he was good at it. However, Nicodemus had a secret. On the inside he wasn't nearly as certain and confident as he appeared on the outside. No matter how he tried, he couldn't deny an inner emptiness that longed to be filled.

In spite of checking the boxes and keeping the rules,
Nicodemus was hungry for something more...
something real...
something life changing.

Have you ever felt that way? Ever longed to be filled? Ever caught yourself going through the motions but sensed there had to be more to life than just checking boxes and keeping rules? Wondered if there's even more to your faith life?

Nicodemus had heard Jesus speak and was taken by His message. The Prophet was not like anyone he had ever met. Jesus spoke of God with casual intimacy and undeniable authority,

3

like He knew Him personally. So, Nicodemus sought Jesus out to learn more, but the Gospel of John tells us he came to Jesus at night... in secret.

You must be reborn.

After introductions, the first words Jesus said to Nicodemus were, "You cannot see the Kingdom of God unless you are born again." Of course, we've heard that phrase so many times it doesn't seem odd to us at all. But put yourself in Nicodemus' place. Nicodemus hadn't even asked a question but is immediately told he simply needs to be "born again."

What an odd and unsettling statement that must have been. The Jewish leader and teacher seemed understandably confused. So, his reasonable follow-up question was something to the effect of, *"Seriously,* go back in my mother and be born again?"

Here is Jesus' response from John's gospel:

> *Jesus answered, "Truly, truly, I say to you, unless one is born of water and the Spirit, he cannot enter the kingdom of God. That which is born of the flesh is flesh, and that which is born of the Spirit is spirit. Do not marvel that I say to you, 'You must be born again.'*
>
> *The wind blows where it wishes, and you hear its sound, but you do not know where it comes from or where it goes. So it is with everyone who is born of the Spirit"* (John 3:5-8).

Jesus is introducing Nicodemus to a new birth into a world that is unseen, invisible, and otherworldly. A world that is spiritual, supernatural, yet absolutely real, invisible to the senses, yet real: this truth is one of the biggest obstacles many people face when it comes to understanding the living, invisible God and walking in His Spirit.

We have been raised to think that only things that are natural or visible are real. Reality is defined by our senses—what we can hear, taste, touch, see, or smell. Yet, Jesus is inviting us into a new birth of the Spirit, which is not natural, but is more real and lasting than anything around us.

Think about it: ours is a spiritual faith which regularly deals with elements that are invisible to our senses, but nonetheless, are very real: things like God, Heaven, Spirit, faith, hope, love, joy, mercy, and grace. It's as though we can accept the concept, but unfortunately, when it comes to stepping out in faith and walking in the Spirit, we struggle just like Nicodemus. We become stuck in the natural, the familiar, and the visible.

You Must be Born Again...

The new birth is our entrance into the Spirit-filled life. The old is gone and the new has come.

- New eyes
- New ears
- New reality
- NEW LIFE

The Wind

In this passage from John 3, Jesus' solution is to simply point Nicodemus (and us) to an unseen reality that we accept and interact with every day: *the wind*. The word translated "wind" is the same word translated Spirit... *pneuma*. It's also the word for *breath*. The wind, the breath, the *pneuma* of the Spirit.

This isn't just a Greek play on words, but a beautiful illustration. You can't see the wind, but you can certainly see what it does. You can feel the wind's effects...

cooling,
 soothing,
  at times a bit unsettling, even scary.

Each time you take a breath, you depend on the unseen to fill and sustain you. The wind isn't visible, but it's real and it's all around us.

The life of the Spirit is just like that. He's real, present, and working all around us. If we'll let the Lord begin to give us eyes of faith, we'll start to see Him in new and amazing ways.

A Journey of the Spirit

As we follow Jesus on this journey with the Holy Spirit, the questions will be:

- *Will we let Him give us new eyes of faith?*
- *Can we open ourselves to the reality of the spiritual, the invisible, even the sometimes unexplainable?*
- *Or will we insist on staying within the safe boundaries of the natural, the predictable, and let's be honest, the controllable?*

Jesus wants you to know that there is more to reality than what you can experience with your natural senses. Jesus invites you to come and see reality as He does.

My prayer, as we walk through these pages together, is that you will be willing to let go and trust the leading of the Spirit. I pray you will grow in your ability to hear His voice and you will experience His infilling in ways you may never have imagined. In the process, may your faith become more real than ever before.

Lord, thank You for that simple illustration of the wind. Help me to become as comfortable with the moving of Your Spirit as I am with the wind. Please help me not to "lean on my own understanding," but to trust You as You call me deeper into the life of the Spirit.

Insight
-2-

MISSING THE POINT

And while staying with them he ordered them not to depart from Jerusalem, but to wait for the promise of the Father, which, he said, "you heard from me; for John baptized with water, but you will be baptized with the Holy Spirit not many days from now." So when they had come together, they asked him, "Lord, will you at this time restore the kingdom to Israel?" He said to them, "It is not for you to know times or seasons that the Father has fixed by his own authority. But you will receive power when the Holy Spirit has come upon you, and you will be my witnesses in Jerusalem and in all Judea and Samaria, and to the end of the earth" (Acts 1:4-8).

RIGHT BEFORE HE ASCENDED TO BE WITH THE Father, Jesus had some important and critical final words for His followers. He told His disciples, "You're going to be baptized with the Holy Spirit and you're going to be endued with power." He had spoken with them about the Spirit before, but this was far more specific and direct. He was leaving them and these were His final instructions. All the promises He'd made,

8

all the things He told them to expect, would be fulfilled in this miraculous provision... the baptism of the Holy Spirit.

From the text, it seems kind of obvious that the disciples are not on the same page as Jesus. It's as though they are distracted and miss what He's actually saying. Their response to this incredible promise was to ask, "Lord, is this the time You're going to restore the kingdom of Israel?" It's almost as if they didn't hear Him because they had something else on their minds. They wanted to know the fate of their nation and what the future held. How much time do we have; what's going to happen?

Now, truth be told, I don't have a lot of room to talk here. I can completely identify with their little rabbit trail. How many times do I find that Jesus is trying to focus my attention on something powerful and life-transforming, but I'm distracted by things that aren't nearly as important and aren't even mine to worry about anyway? Sometimes, it's easier to see these things in someone else than in myself.

In the passage above, there is an obvious disconnect between what the disciples wanted to know and what Jesus knew they needed to know. They wanted to know about the future, but Jesus was saying, "Don't worry about the future, I've got that covered. What I really want you to know is that I am going to baptize you, fill you, immerse you in My Spirit, and it is going to be so powerful it will change everything!"

Every day, we read or hear of people lamenting the lack of real power in the church today. There does seem to be an obvious disparity between what we read in the pages of the Bible and what many of us experience in our Christian life. Could it be that, like them, we too are so focused on things that are less important that we completely overlook the most important thing? I think Jesus is spelling out for them, and for us, the most important thing.

I'm afraid our greatest disconnect is our failure to seek and surrender to the infilling of the Holy Spirit.

Some people get really weird about the doctrinal issues surrounding the infilling of the Spirit, but I'm obviously not talking about doctrine here. I'm talking about the actual experience of infilling. His Spirit, resident in us, speaking, leading, empowering, and moving through us just like Jesus promised. This is the actual essence of our salvation.

We understand and give thanks for the cross, but the cross is not the point of our faith. It is *the essential doorway* through which we must walk, but the point is the infilling presence of the Lord.

The point is fellowship with the Father.

The reason for the cross is that God created us for fellowship with Him, but sin separated us from what we were created for—daily, vibrant, eternal, spiritual communion with Him. Jesus' sacrifice on the cross paid the death penalty for our sin, opening the door to a relationship with our Father. So, the minute we reduce Christ's work on the cross to nothing more than a contract where our penalty is paid so we can receive grace, we miss the whole point of our salvation.

Our salvation is **not** simply legal.
Our salvation is **primarily** relational.

Our salvation **is** the person of God's Holy Spirit **resident** in us.

Our salvation is not simply the legal satisfaction of the law's requirements, as important as that is, but rather the opening of the door to the person of God's Holy Spirit so He can reside in us. We often act like justification is the end of our salvation, but it's not; it's the beginning! It is then that God fills us with His Spirit and begins to set us free from the chains of sin and death. The minute we surrender to Christ as Savior, we are saved and set free, but set free to what? We are set free to life in the Spirit. The Apostle Paul says it powerfully and succinctly:

> *You, however, are not in the flesh but in the Spirit, if in fact the Spirit of God dwells in you. Anyone who does not have the Spirit of Christ does not belong to Him. But if Christ is in you, although the body is dead because of sin, the Spirit is life because of righteousness. If the Spirit of Him who raised Jesus from the dead dwells in you, He who raised Christ Jesus from the dead will also give life to your mortal bodies through His Spirit who dwells in you* (Romans 8:9-11).

He makes it perfectly clear that the life of Christ cannot happen in us without the abiding presence of the Holy Spirit. So, how are you doing when it comes to interacting with the very Spirit of God who lives in you? He is with you every moment of every day. Do you see His presence as a close personal friendship to be cultivated? Are you talking with Him, listening for Him, and including Him in your discussions and decisions?

My prayer is that these few paragraphs serve as an invitation to press into the infilling of the Holy Spirit. Ask God to reveal areas where you are allowing other things to "fill" you. Invite the Father to take you beyond doctrine to the true experience of abiding in His presence.

Lord, thank You for the gift of Your Spirit in me. Help me to include You in every part of my life. Help me to hear and respond to Your call to press in and to be immersed more deeply in the things of the Spirit than ever before. I pray according to Romans 8 that it would be Your Spirit that would truly give life to my mortal body as You live through me.

Insight
-3-

LEARNING TO FLY

For all who are led by the Spirit of God are sons of God. For you did not receive the spirit of slavery to fall back into fear but you have received the Spirit of adoption as sons, by whom we cry, "Abba. Father." The Spirit himself bears witness with our spirit that we are children of God, and if children, then heirs—heirs of God and fellow heirs with Christ, provided we suffer with him in order that we may also be glorified with him (Romans 8:14-17).

STOP FOR A MOMENT TO CONSIDER THE IMPLICA-tions of God's Spirit actually inhabiting a person. The very Spirit of the eternal Creator resident in us. The phrase Paul uses is, "gives life to your mortal bodies." Jesus promised a different kind of power that believers would receive from His Spirit. This reality is unbelievably exciting when you stop to consider its implications!

The infilling of the Spirit initiates a fundamental change in the nature of the new believer. We are completely different because of His work in our lives. The scripture's teachings on this are abundantly clear. However, it seems like some of this has been lost in recent years. In fact, over the last few decades, many in the church have inadvertently downplayed this transformation in the name of "cultural relevance."

Cultural relevance is the very important idea that for the church to be effective, we must be relevant to the culture we're trying to reach. If not, we end up talking to ourselves and answering questions no one is asking. This much is certainly true and worth remembering. But a problem arises when we cross that fine line between clearly speaking the gospel in a way the world can relate to and becoming like the world in a misguided effort to reach them. We don't want to "scare them off," so we downplay, or soft sell, the parts of the Gospel that seem radical or too "out there." Nowhere is this more evident than with the infilling of the Holy Spirit.

When describing the work of the Spirit, Jesus used the illustration of the wind (John 3:5-8). You can't see the wind, but you know it's there and you can see and hear what it does.

For just a moment imagine an eagle, who flies by harnessing the power of the wind. When you watch an eagle soar, you are not watching a solo performance, but rather witnessing a dance between two partners—the eagle and the wind. What a beautiful picture of the Spirit-filled life! Now imagine this eagle agreeing to teach some "non-fliers" how to fly. In an effort to be culturally relevant, our eagle friend comes and walks among us, so we can relate. He talks about flying, he gives classes in flying, he even writes songs about flying, but, oddly, he never actually flies or challenges us to fly because the wind might be too scary or "out there" for the uninitiated. Before long, we're all walking and squawking like eagles, but no one is really flying. In fact, over time, even our eagle friend forgets how to fly and settles for writing books about the doctrine of flying.

That may seem like just a ridiculous illustration until we compare the Spirit-filled life, described in the pages of scripture, to what we see in much of Christianity today. Where is the power that is so evident in the New Testament? How are we doing at "rising up with wings like eagles" (Isaiah 40:31)? We are empowered to fly in the Spirit. How's it going? The truth is, cultural relevance kind of breaks down when we're talking about moving in the power of the unseen Spirit of God!

Life in the Spirit is not just a different lifestyle, a cleaner morality, or a new set of rules. The infilling of the Spirit fundamentally changes us.

According to Romans 8, because of the Spirit's presence:

- We are made alive and set free. Our spirit, which was dead in sin, is brought to life and awakened by His Spirit.
- We are the children of God. We have a literal (not physical, but literal) transformation of our spiritual DNA as we are adopted into His family. We are given a new spirit, a new identity, and a new name in Him.
- We become heirs with Jesus of an amazing inheritance as sons and daughters of the King.
- We are empowered to live the life of Christ. The Spirit-filled life is not about me doing my best for Jesus, but rather the Spirit of Jesus living through me.
- We have the assurance that we are the children of God. According to Romans 8, the assurance of the believer is not simply some mental principle that we recite over and over. The assurance of the believer is the actual Spirit of God with us, moving, acting, interceding, and reminding us of who we are in Christ.

The Spirit-filled life is a journey of radical transformation. Don't settle for a watered-down version of the real thing. Press in daily! Invite Him to speak and then follow in obedience. See if the Spirit doesn't lead you to heights you may never have seen before. As you follow His lead, don't be surprised if you begin to realize you are flying.

Lord, please help me to reject fear and the status quo. I want the fullness of Your Spirit at work in me—growing, leading, empowering, and transforming. Flying in the Spirit may seem a little out of sync with the world around me and people may not understand. Deliver me from the fear of men and help me to look for approval from only You.

Insight
-4-

Becoming Like Him

For those whom He foreknew, He also predes-
tined to be conformed to the image of His Son,
in order that he might be the firstborn among
many brothers (Romans 8:29).

For this reason, I bow my knees before the Father,
from whom every family in heaven and on
earth is named, that according to the riches of
His glory, He may grant you to be strengthened
with power through His Spirit in your inner being
(Ephesians 3:14-16).

ONE OF THE GREAT CHALLENGES OF OUR FAITH IS
the call to be like Jesus. It is the core idea behind the labels
"Christian" or "Christ-follower." Romans 8:29 says that we are
destined to be conformed to the image of Christ.

As I read about Jesus in the Scriptures, this challenge can
be both exciting and discouraging. Jesus is the most beautiful
and amazing person to ever walk the planet. He is holy. He is
loving beyond description. He is full of grace and truth. Which,
of course, seems impossible to us in our current cultural understanding. You're either a person who leans toward grace or
toward truth. However, Jesus isn't 50/50 grace and truth. He's

100/100 and the most gracious and truthful person ever—both at the same time. We haven't even mentioned that He walked on water and raised the dead!

The idea of being like Jesus is both wonderful and seemingly impossible. That's why so many believers just give up. They try, fail, and throw up their hands in surrender. Ironically, in that moment, they have stumbled upon one of the greatest truths of the Spirit-filled life.

We can't become like Jesus on our own and we're not supposed to. One of the many gifts that God's Spirit brings into the life of the believer is the power to live like Jesus. Take a moment to carefully read Romans 8:7-11. The Apostle Paul bluntly states that the power to please God and walk like Jesus can only come from the Holy Spirit. The flesh *can't* do it. It's impossible. In the flesh, I can try to be like Jesus, but without the presence and power of the Spirit, it's not going to happen. It is His presence in us that gives us His power. That's what Jesus was pointing out in Luke 24:49 when He said, "Behold, I am sending the promise of my Father upon you but stay in the city until you are clothed with power from on high."

Immersed in Him

"Between the time of Christ's resurrection and ascension, and the time when the world was being turned upside down by the apostles (Acts 17:6), stands Pentecost— the baptism of the Holy Spirit. What transformed the apostles from timid witnesses to mighty saints? Simply this— the baptism of the Holy Spirit. Are you tired of living a powerless Christian life? Encounter the Spirit and His baptism in your life."

– Larry Keefauver [2]

I Give Up.

Unfortunately, because we can't live this new life in our own strength, many believers give up rather than trusting the Spirit to empower them. In a distorted application of the doctrine of grace (see Romans 6:1-2), many simply proclaim, "This is who I am, I trust God will forgive me." While His grace surely provides for the forgiveness of all who repent, His grace also provides the power to walk in new life... the life of Christ.

One of our biggest struggles is we often live as though there is no power. See Ephesians 3:14-16 above. Our lack of power is not because of the Spirit. It's because of our failure to seek and surrender to the infilling of the Holy Spirit.

Every Christ-follower should be growing, transforming, and becoming more like Jesus. Those who are filled should experience victory. Those who have the Spirit should be overcomers. Those who are filled with the Spirit should manifest the presence and the power of Jesus. You and I should live like Jesus because the exact same Spirit that lived in Jesus lives in us.

Paul wraps up his thoughts in Ephesians 3 this way: "Now to him who is able to do far more abundantly than all that we ask or think, according to the power at work within us, to him be the glory and the church and in Christ Jesus throughout all generations, forever and ever. Amen" (Ephesians 3:20-21).

I'd like you to take a moment of reflection. Whatever you may have imagined or asked for in the context of your spiritual life is much smaller than what God can and will do for those who are filled with His Spirit. Whatever you've prayed for is less than what God desires for you. Stop and think about the things that you've hardly dared to hope for. Think about those situations in your life you thought were too difficult or the people you thought were too broken. Imagine somebody you love and care about, but you've almost lost hope that they could ever surrender and turn to Christ.

According to the passage we just read, there is a power working in you by which God is able to do more than we could ask or think. One of the great tragedies of our faith is that we pray and dream too small. We're filled with the same Spirit that raised Jesus from the dead. We should expect supernatural power and expect the work of the Spirit to be supernatural in our lives.

**You and I have been empowered to live like Jesus.
What's stopping us?**

Lord, I am so grateful for the gift of Your Spirit. You didn't give me an impossible task or set of rules; You gave me Your presence, leading, guiding, and empowering. In the quiet of this moment, I surrender to Your leadership through Your Spirit in me. Help me to see differently, pray differently, and walk differently as I follow You each day. Make me more like Jesus.

Insight
-5-

FILLED WITH LOVE

That according to the riches of his glory he may grant you to be strengthened with power through his Spirit in your inner being, so that Christ may dwell in your hearts through faith— that you, being rooted and grounded in love, may have strength to comprehend with all the saints what is the breadth and length and height and depth, and to know the love of Christ that surpasses knowledge, that you may be filled with all the fullness of God (Ephesians 3:16-19).

SOMETHING STRANGE HAS HAPPENED IN CULTURE and even within Christianity over the last decade or so. With the saturation of social media, everyone has a myriad of opinions as well as a platform to comment on. As people have run with their own daily op-ed columns, they say things in public (yes, social media is public) they never would have said before. The conversations have become increasingly caustic, emulating the tone of the larger media around us. There is a growing adversarial cloud of "meanness" enveloping the public discourse.

This is particularly disturbing as it pertains to followers of Jesus. We are the people who profess to serve a God of love and are to be known by our love for one another. Instead, there

21

is a growing sector of professed believers who seem to think it is their duty to criticize and put down the rest of their brothers and sisters in the church. Something is seriously wrong when followers of Jesus are abandoning their love for one another to join in on the "gotcha" mentality of the world around us.

That's when we know we're listening to the wrong voices.
Or worse yet, maybe we're walking in the wrong spirit.

In the passage above, Paul talks about the relationship between the Spirit's infilling and the love of Christ in the life of the believer. He lays out three beautiful and very distinct ways that the Spirit manifests God's love in each of us.

First, Paul says that because of the power of the Spirit, which is the Spirit of Jesus in us, we are rooted and grounded in love. Love is to be the very soil in which our lives grow. Without it, we lack the proper environment to mature as Christ-followers. As we look around us, our responses of rejoicing, grief, or even righteous anger should all come from a place of love. What Paul is saying is that because of the Spirit, love gradually becomes our paradigm, the atmosphere of our lives, and the very foundation that we work from.

Next, he points out that the Spirit empowers us to comprehend the vastness of God's amazing love. This is a bigger challenge than most people realize. Comprehending the love of God in a broken world is no small thing. Most of what we see around us is human love that says, "If you do something for me, then I'll love you." This is conditional love, and for many of us, it's all we've ever known. When we're presented with the idea of a God who loves us unconditionally, it's hard to find a framework for such a love and we end up filling in the blanks with our own experience and understanding. As a result, many people's view of the Father is distorted because they just can't envision what real love looks like. Paul says the Spirit opens our eyes and our minds so that we begin to comprehend the breadth, length, height, and depth of our Father's amazing love.

Finally, it's important to note that Paul doesn't simply say we'll comprehend the love of God. No, he says we will comprehend and "know" the love of God. In other words, we'll understand and experience it. You see, I can study the love of God or I can write wonderful papers on the love of God, but if I've never received and experienced it for myself, it will be nothing more than a theory or a nice ideal. I will never be able to truly grasp or share my Father's amazing love.

Receive His Love

Before I can ever truly walk in the love of Jesus Christ, I have to let His Spirit fill me and receive His love personally. I have to personally receive His forgiveness. I have to experience His grace for myself. I have to come to the place that when I think about God's love, it is so real it brings tears to my eyes and I struggle for words. That's what it's like to really know the inexpressible love of God.

This is how the lawyer, turned evangelist, Charles Finney described his encounter with the incredible love of God: *"I could feel the impression like a wave of electricity, going through and through me. Indeed, it seemed to come in waves and waves of liquid love—for I could not express it any other way. It seemed like the very breath of God. I can recollect distinctly that it seemed to fan me, like immense wings. No words can express the wonderful love that was shed abroad in my heart. I wept aloud with joy and love."–Memoirs of Charles G. Finney* [3]

Our Father loves you like you've never been loved before. What's even more amazing is that He has placed His Spirit in you, as a follower of Jesus, to personally love you and develop His love in you. This simple truth, lived out in the life of Spirit-filled believers, has the power to radically change the church and ultimately change the world!

Lord, thank You for Your amazing, unconditional love for me. Thank You that You never let go, You never turn Your back on me, and Your love never fails. Forgive me for forgetting and for sometimes operating from a paradigm of fear. I am loved by You and filled with Your Spirit of love. Help me to see the world around me through Your eyes and to respond in Your love.

Insight
-6-

WISDOM AND UNDERSTANDING

*There shall come forth a shoot from the stump
of Jesse and a branch from his root shall bear
fruit. And the Spirit of the Lord shall rest upon
him, the Spirit of wisdom and understanding*
(Isaiah 11:1-2).

I SAT LISTENING TO AN INTERVIEW ON A NEWS
program the other day and was having a difficult time not
throwing something in frustration. The conversation was
about some current national issue and the foolishness being
presented was shocking. It was as though history had never
happened and reality didn't exist. Here was a person being presented as an authority or expert, advocating ideas and actions
that were demonstrably foolish and void of wisdom.

Unfortunately, I wish I could say this was a unique experience. As more and more people reject the Creator and the truth
of His creation, wisdom seems to be one of the great casual-
ties. Even an alarming number of Christians, under increasing
pressure to conform to culture, are rejecting wisdom in favor
of the popular opinions of the day. Wisdom is increasingly in
short supply, but it doesn't have to be.

The good news is God promises to give wisdom to anyone
who will ask (James 1:5). In fact, if we understand the infilling

25

of the Spirit, we have the greatest source of wisdom in the universe already at our disposal.

According to Isaiah 11:1-2, the Spirit of God, which would come to rest on Jesus at His baptism, was the Spirit of wisdom and understanding. This is the same Spirit who resides in, and empowers, you and me.

Take a moment to really consider the implications of this truth...

The Gift of Wisdom...

- His Spirit of Wisdom resides in every Spirit-filled believer.

- Begin to pray daily for the humility to listen and the courage to follow.

Are you currently facing any challenges where you need greater wisdom?

Do you, right now, have any dicey relational situations that require divine understanding?

Would you like the wisdom and understanding to discern God's will or direction today?

The same Spirit that gave wisdom and understanding to Jesus resides in you.

Jesus laid this out for His disciples in John 16:12-15. As you hear what He tells them, keep in mind that these are the ones who had seen Him walk on water. They handed out the loaves and fishes when Jesus fed the multitude. They had witnessed the miraculous firsthand. Even to these, He said in verse 12, "There is more I have to tell you, but you can't bear it right now."

In other words, as much as you've seen so far, there is more. There's more I want to reveal to you, but you are not ready. He doesn't stop there; He adds, "But when the Spirit of truth comes, He will guide you in all truth."

So, as you grow and mature, God will continue to give you truth and continue to reveal what He has for you through the Spirit.

> "When the Spirit of truth comes, he will guide you into all the truth, for He will not speak on his own authority, but whatever he hears he will speak, and he will declare to you the things that are to come. He will glorify me, for he will take what is mine and declare it to you. All that the Father has is mine. Therefore, I said that he will take what is mine and declare it to you" (John 16:13-15).

Jesus is saying the Spirit of truth will personally guide you, He will personally lead you, and He will give you everything Jesus has for you. One of the great gifts of the Spirit in us is the gift of wisdom. The beauty of this gift is that it yields amazing fruit in every area of life. Imagine your character, relationships, business, finances, and ministry all being transformed and blessed because of walking in the Spirit's wisdom.

However, one word of caution. In the spirit of full disclosure, you should be aware that as the Spirit gives you wisdom and you begin to walk in it, you will regularly be walking in complete opposition to the world's wisdom. Read Paul's warning in 1 Corinthians 3:18-19:

Do not deceive yourselves. If any of you think you are wise by the standards of this age, you should become "fools" so that you may become wise. For the wisdom of this world is foolishness in God's sight....

The more you grow in wisdom, the more you may feel out of sync with the ever-increasing foolishness of the world around us. Don't expect people to understand or applaud. When wisdom leads you to swim upstream against the current of popularity, remember the words of A.W. Tozer, who said, "The masses are always wrong." [4]

Wisdom is an incredible gift of God's Spirit. Because of His abiding presence, you will know what to do and you'll have the power to do it. If you've ever known a person of true wisdom, you know what a beautiful thing it is.

Lord, when You walked on this earth, You were filled with the Spirit of wisdom and under-standing and You've filled me with that same Spirit, Your Spirit. Thank You for the gift of wisdom. Teach me to slow down and listen for Your voice of wisdom before I act. Help me to see the world, people, and circumstances through Your eyes and respond as You would.

Insight
-7-

NEVER THIRST AGAIN

Everyone who drinks this water will be thirsty again,
but whoever drinks the water I give them will never thirst.
—Jesus

JOHN CHAPTER 4 TELLS A BEAUTIFUL STORY IN
which Jesus surprises a woman by simply asking for a drink.
He meets her while resting at a well, near the city of Sychar, in
Samaria, where she is coming to draw water. But there is something different about how and when she comes. It is during the
heat of the day and alone, almost as if she is avoiding the other
women who come there each morning.

When Jesus first speaks, His simple request for a drink
catches her off guard because everyone knows that Jews and
Samaritans don't associate, particularly a Jewish man with a
Samaritan woman. When she says as much, He gives an unusual
response, with what I imagine to be a compassionate and yet
somewhat mischievous smile, "If you knew the gift that God
had in store and who you were talking to, you'd ask me for a
drink and I'd give you living water."

Well, this just confuses her even more because she can see
that He doesn't have anything with which to draw water. But
then Jesus reveals the gift.

*Everyone who drinks this water will be thirsty
again, but whoever drinks the water I give them
will never thirst. Indeed, the water I give them
will become in them a spring of water welling up
to eternal life* (John 4:13-14 NIV).

As John relates the story, he makes it clear that the woman still has no clue what the Lord is really talking about.

**The problem is she thinks that Jesus is talking about water
when He's actually talking about thirst.**

In the Bible, thirst and hunger are regularly used as metaphors to describe the longing of the heart—that deep, hidden thirst of the soul that each of us possesses and will often spend our entire lives trying to satisfy. This natural thirst is given to us by God in order to draw us to Him, but unfortunately, we go to all kinds of other "wells" to be filled. Consider how often we run after things like success, wealth, possessions, adventure, entertainment, and even unhealthy relationships in an attempt to fill the longing of our hearts.

With the woman at the well, Jesus turns the conversation to the thirst of her soul with one simple request, "Go get your husband," to which she replies she doesn't have a husband. Jesus matter-of-factly says, "You're right, you don't have a husband," and then goes on to reveal the fact that she'd had five husbands and was living with prospect number six. She had been going from one unhealthy relationship to another in a series of vain attempts to be filled.

What did she feel in that moment of revelation?
With one request, Jesus laid bare the thirst of her soul.
What would Jesus say to reveal the thirst of your soul?

Jesus had offered a thirsty woman living water so that she would never thirst again. John tells us that she joyfully accepted His offer and actually convinced many others in Sychar to do the same! A few chapters later in John 7, we see a beautiful connection and discover what the water actually is:

> *On the last and greatest day of the festival, Jesus stood and said in a loud voice, "Let anyone who is thirsty come to me and drink. Whoever believes in me, as Scripture has said, rivers of living water will flow from within them." By this he meant the Spirit, whom those who believed in him were later to receive. Up to that time the Spirit had not been given, since Jesus had not yet been glorified* (John 7:37-39 NIV).

The living water that quenches the thirst
of our soul is His Spirit living in us.

Jesus describes the Spirit as rivers of living water flowing from within the life of the believer. He is the only one who can truly and deeply satisfy. Sadly, many people, even believers, run around frantically trying to be filled by other things, but as Jesus points out, with any other water you will always thirst again.

*You can drink at the fountain of wealth, **but you will thirst again.***

*You can drink from the fountain of fame, **but you will thirst again.***

*You can try to quench your thirst with pleasure, achievement, education, sex, and even human love, **but you will thirst again.***

**Only the infilling of the Holy Spirit
satisfies the longing of our hearts.**

Only those who are filled with the Spirit will find what their heart has been longing for and have their thirst truly quenched. It's like a perpetual fountain that continually springs up and keeps springing up from within. The Spirit is an incredible gift of the Father. However, as I write this, my heart is heavy for believers who profess faith in Christ, but never seem to be filled. Those who appear to understand salvation but also seem to lack the abundance, contentment, and fulfillment that comes from being filled with His Spirit.

In reflection...

- *How full do you feel in the Spirit?*
- *Do you still find yourself trying to go to other wells to quench your thirst?*
- *If so, what is keeping you from truly seeking and surrendering to the infilling of the Spirit and having your thirst quenched, never to thirst again?*

Jesus gave His Spirit to overflow in us as a continual well of love, acceptance, peace, joy, and hope, filling and satisfying the deepest longing of our heart. Take a moment right now to receive the living water that is yours in the Spirit.

Father, please fill me with Your Holy Spirit! Forgive me for the times I tried to let other things fill me up. Let my heart find its deep satisfaction in You and You alone. I know now that the only way to quench the deep thirst within me is through Your gift of Your Spirit. Thank You for this powerful and wonderful provision.

Insight
-8-

BEING FILLED

And while staying with them he ordered them not to depart from Jerusalem, but to wait for the promise of the Father, which, he said, "you heard from me; for John baptized with water, but you will be baptized with the Holy Spirit not many days from now" (Acts 1:4-5).

And they were all filled with the Holy Spirit and began to speak in other tongues as the Spirit gave them utterance (Acts 2:4).

And when they had prayed, the place in which they were gathered together was shaken, and they were all filled with the Holy Spirit and continued to speak the word of God with boldness (Acts 4:31).

THE INFILLING OF THE SPIRIT IS AN ONGOING, daily encounter with the presence of the living God. This daily experience is an absolute game-changer that radically transforms the life of a Christ-follower! The gift of the infilling is the source of New Testament power that true believers long for.

If this is truly something so powerful and so critical, why do we hardly ever talk about it? When was the last time you heard teaching on how or why to be filled with the Holy Spirit? I'm afraid the enemy of our souls has cleverly used the imbalance and abuses of a few to marginalize this wonderful dimension of our faith.

I think much of this comes from the fact that the infilling of the Holy Spirit has been the subject of controversy within certain Christian circles. There are those who believe that you are completely filled with the Spirit at salvation and those who teach that there is a second experience of greater infilling, sometimes called the baptism of the Holy Spirit. These two "camps" have created a dynamic where many pastors and congregations simply avoid the subject for fear of being wrong, offensive, or divisive.

What if both ideas are actually true,
even if they also somewhat miss the point?

Jesus commanded His followers to wait in Jerusalem until they were baptized with the Holy Spirit. They did as He instructed; Acts 2 records their first encounter, saying they were all "filled" with the Holy Spirit. Then in Acts 4, after Peter and John were released from prison, we're told of a powerful prayer meeting where the entire place was shaken with the power of God and they were all "filled" with the Spirit, again. So, we see many of the same people, including Peter and John, filled in Acts 2 and then again in Acts 4.

What if the infilling does involve a second experience,
and a third, and a fourth, and so on?

35

In Romans 8:9, the Apostle Paul made it clear that every believer receives the Spirit at salvation;

> *You, however, are not in the flesh but in the Spirit,*
> *if in fact the Spirit of God dwells in you. Anyone*
> *who does not have the Spirit of Christ does not*
> *belong to him.*

The Scripture says we clearly receive the infilling of the Spirit at salvation. However, based on what we see in Acts, we should also pursue a second experience of infilling and a third, fourth, etc...

The infilling is an ongoing daily encounter with the Spirit of God in the life of the believer.

One of my favorite Bible verses regarding being filled with the Spirit is Ephesians 5:18, which basically says, 'Don't be drunk with wine, because that will ruin your life. Instead, be filled with the Holy Spirit.' Aside from the sheer wisdom of not drinking too much, this gives us a beautiful picture of what being filled really is. Where I grew up in Illinois, when someone is arrested for drunk driving, they are cited for DUI or "driving under the influence". The danger, of course, is that a person who is drunk is under the influence or control of alcohol. What Paul is saying is don't do that; instead, be under the influence or control of the Spirit. That's what being filled is all about.

Greater levels of infilling are released as I walk in greater levels of surrender to the influence and control of the Spirit of God. In truth, the continued infilling is not about me getting more of the Spirit, but the Spirit getting more of me.

Every day, you and I have a choice regarding whom we will listen to and whom we will follow. Paul lays that choice out clearly:

> *Those who live according to the flesh have their minds set on what the flesh desires; but those who live in accordance with the Spirit have their minds set on what the Spirit desires. The mind governed by the flesh is death, but the mind governed by the Spirit is life and peace* (Romans 8:5-6 NIV).

Our sin nature and even our upbringing have trained us to be led by the flesh, which results in death. However, because of the infilling, you and I have the potential, in every situation, to respond in the Spirit. Paul points out that the choice I make between Spirit and flesh will determine what I experience—either death or life and peace. The sobering reality is that by disregarding the Spirit, I have the potential to literally quench the Holy Spirit like a water hose dousing a roaring fire. If I choose to listen for the Spirit, follow the Spirit, and be filled with the Spirit, I will begin to walk in the Spirit-filled life and experience the power that His presence brings!

I want to encourage you to reject the dry, stale, empty existence that so many seem to settle for. This is not the life the Scripture describes, and it's definitely not what you were made for! You were created by a loving Father to be filled with His presence and His power. You were created to soar on eagles' wings! The secret is to daily surrender to the voice and moving of the Spirit in you.

For reflection:

- *Are you hungry to truly exhibit God's supernatural presence in your life every day, or have you settled for something less?*
- *If you began to follow the Spirit's leading more closely, what are some things that might change?*
- *Jot down a few ways that you would like to more fully surrender to the infilling of God's Spirit.*
- *Why not begin today?*

Thank You, Father, for Your abiding presence. Teach me to be under the influence of Your Spirit, rather than the flesh. Fill me daily as I follow Your voice and surrender to Your leadership. Thank You that You continually supply all that I need to fulfill the mission You have called me to fulfill on earth.

Part Two: A New Life

Earthly wisdom is doing what comes naturally.
Godly wisdom is doing what the Holy Spirit compels us to do.
- Charles Stanley [5]

If we live by the Spirit, let us also keep in step with the Spirit.
(Galatians 5:25)

Insight
-9-

FALSE ADVERTISING

We were therefore buried with him through baptism into death in order that, just as Christ was raised from the dead through the glory of the Father, we too may live a new life (Romans 6:4 NIV).

Have you ever been the victim of false advertising?

WE HAVE SOME GAS STATIONS AROUND OUR CITY that drew me in several times with what turned out to be a bait and switch. You would see their sign advertising really good prices, drive in and get ready to fill up your car, only to realize that their gas prices were not really their gas prices. Oh, you could get their posted price, but only if you paid for a carwash as well. Otherwise, your price would be this much higher price over here. They might as well post a sign on the pump that says, "Gotcha!" The first time I took the bait, I was pretty excited. As I pulled in, I thought, "Look at that gas price," only to be disappointed by their *real* price per gallon. Like any self-respecting price shopper, I got back in my car and drove to the station down the street. It's a matter of principle.

I wonder if people ever feel a sense of false advertising with what they see in much of the Christian world today. You know...

41

a gap between the claims of the brochure and the reality of the product. Unfortunately, I've talked with more than a few unbelieving people who just don't buy it. They have been exposed to the idea of the Gospel and even heard about Jesus. However, based on encounters with some professing Christians, they have come away feeling like the actual product is lacking. I realize that there's more to these stories than what's being presented, but they do have an uncomfortable ring of truth.

Let's go one step further. If we're really honest, I wonder how many times *we* as followers of Jesus may have felt something similar. The Bible paints a powerful picture of Spirit-filled believers living a new life in Christ. What about those who feel like the claims presented in scripture and sermons don't match their experience? Even a Christian might end up feeling discouraged or almost duped. I've actually heard disappointed believers say things like, "I tried it and it didn't work."

Let me pause for a moment to ask you...

Do you sometimes feel like something is missing?

Do you ever hear other people's testimonies and feel left out?

What about the powerful claims that we read about in the Gospels?

Are you experiencing the new life promised to us as Christ-followers?

Product Failure versus User Error

I'd like to suggest that what we're facing here is not a faulty product, but rather user error. The problem is not the Gospel, but rather the misguided attempt to embrace the Gospel without interrupting our self-directed, modern life. The idea of a gospel without cost, where I get to continue living my life, my way, is a gross distortion of our faith and will always lack spiritual vitality. Look at what Jesus said when He promised His followers power:

> *"But you will receive power when the Holy Spirit has come upon you, and you will be my witnesses in Jerusalem and in all Judea and Samaria, and to the end of the earth"* (Acts 1:8).

The power of the Christian life is found in the infilling presence of the Spirit of God. Remember, being filled with the Spirit means to be under His influence and control. Submission to His leadership will always result in a new life and the power we read about in the New Testament.

Salesmen versus Satisfied Customers

Jesus said one of the great results of this power is that we will be His witnesses. Witness is a word that has been brutalized in many church circles. We've changed the word to mean presenting a canned gospel presentation to a willing (or unwilling) audience. When I was in high school, our youth group would load up a van and go into a neighborhood and "witness." We'd knock on doors and ask people if they knew where they'd go if they died that night. You'd get arrested for that today!

The sad fact is that many of us were taught to share the Gospel like salesmen, when what Jesus described is far more like a satisfied customer. No offense to salespeople, but no one wants to hear a sales pitch. However, we all like the recommendation of a satisfied customer. That's why we love reviews from Amazon, Google, and Yelp. What Jesus was talking about was more like a witness in a courtroom. A witness is simply someone who tells what they've seen or experienced—a lot like a satisfied customer.

The Role of a Witness

A Witness simply tells what he or she has seen...

- What have you seen God do in and around you?

- How could your eyewitness testimony open someone's eyes to the goodness and power of God?

His power in us transforms every part of our lives. Witnessing is simply sharing what we've seen His power accomplish in, through, and around us. We love to share our positive experiences, and in fact, we do it all the time. Witnessing is sharing my story of what the Lord has done in my life.

Of course, what this means is that being an effective witness starts with having an actual experience with His Spirit. You can't witness to what you haven't seen. The Scripture says, "Taste and see that the Lord is good," and that's where an authentic testimony begins. When your life has been truly impacted by the presence of God, all you have to do is share what He has done. When you are filled with the Spirit and walking in His power, your testimony is compelling. Your story of actually seeing God move is powerful!

People may ultimately reject your testimony, but it will never be confused with false advertising.

My prayer is that you genuinely experience the power that accompanies the Spirit-filled life; and your testimony would be the story of His miraculous presence at work in you, and would draw others to Him.

Thank You, Father, for Your promise of power through the Spirit. I'm hungry for the new life You describe in Your Word! Help me to be so filled with Your Spirit that You live through me. May my life be a testimony of Your transforming grace to those around me.

Insight
-10-

THREE LAWS

So I find it to be a law that when I want to do right, evil lies close at hand. For I delight in the law of God, in my inner being, but I see in my members another law waging war against the law of my mind and making me captive to the law of sin that dwells in my members. Wretched man that I am! Who will deliver me from this body of death? Thanks be to God through Jesus Christ our Lord. So then, I myself serve the law of God with my mind, but with my flesh I serve the law of sin (Romans 7:21-25).

Wretched man that I am!

MOST OF US CAN RELATE IN ONE WAY OR ANOTHER to Paul's frustrated confession of brokenness. I know I can. I vividly remember being in animated conversations (that's what we call fights) with my wife, Lauri, and saying things that I knew were not kind, helpful, or wise. What's worse is there was a voice inside of me, like a good friend, telling me as much and begging me to stop! It's as though there were two voices inside me. One was advocating for what is right and one was advocating for what felt gratifying in the moment. I don't think either

Paul or I are schizophrenic, but there is definitely a serious tug-o-war going on. Maybe you can relate.

Paul refers to these voices, or leanings, as laws. There is the law of God etched on the heart of every human being. It is the part of us that knows right from wrong. We may call it conscience, but it is really that part of all of us that knows we are created for a higher purpose. Earlier in Romans 7, Paul uses the illustration of covetousness. He says without God's law, we wouldn't even know it's wrong to covet. Without God's law, we'd be like a dog just waiting for the chance to steal another dog's bone. If you've ever had two dogs and just one bone, you know this story. Of course, we don't blame a thieving dog when at first opportunity he takes the bone and runs for it. No, we expect it, because it's instinct. He doesn't know any better because he doesn't have the law of God written on his heart. However, we do, and consequently something in us does know right from wrong. We have this standard because it is part of God's law.

Paul's deep frustration stems from the fact that there is also another law at work, which he calls the law of sin. This is the law that says, "It may be wrong, but I'm going to do it anyway." We may know that it's wrong to gossip, but we do it anyway. We know it's wrong to take that thing that isn't ours, or berate that person, or use another person to get what we want, or watch that film, or look at that website, or lie on that form, and the list goes on. We know it's wrong, but we choose to do it anyway. I don't know if there is any greater evidence of the existence of these two laws than our tendency to justify our sinful actions. If someone else does it, it's wrong, but if we do it, well, there was a good reason. We acknowledge the standard; we just don't keep it.

Interestingly, when talking about covetousness, Paul says, "But sin, seizing an opportunity through the commandment, produced in me all kinds of covetousness." This is an interesting revelation. What he seems to be saying is that the root of the sin nature is fundamentally rebellion. In other words, the commandment gave the rebellious sin nature something to rebel against.

So, Paul finds himself trapped between two laws which are at work within him: God's law which upholds right and wrong, and the law of sin which rebels against God's law. Take a moment to re-read his exasperation in the verses at the beginning of this chapter.

If this was where he left us, we would all just have to live in the frustrating tension between knowing what is right and being powerless to do it. Thankfully, he didn't stop there. His next words give us incredible hope.

> *Therefore, there is now no condemnation for those who are in Christ Jesus, because through Christ Jesus the law of the Spirit who gives life has set you free from the law of sin and death* (Romans 8:1-2).

Did you catch that? No, not just the "no condemnation" part (although that is awesome!), the other part—the part about the law. It's true, we all are caught in this struggle between two laws, but Paul just introduced a *third* law—the law of the Spirit. This third law is a game-changer and is God's amazing provision for every believer. We aren't left as helpless victims trying to live the new life in our own strength. We have been given the Spirit of God to empower us.

Stop and think about this for a moment. We don't have to live with the shame and frustration of knowing God's law but being helpless to keep it. He has come to live in each believer, bringing about the life we were created for. In Him, we know what to do and have the power to do it.

When Orville and Wilber Wright first envisioned flying, people thought they'd lost their minds. Everyone knew that humans couldn't fly because of the law of gravity. While there was something within them that longed to soar high above the earth, they knew they had to deal with gravity. So, the Wright brothers designed a wing system which allowed them to harness the power of the wind to create lift. This lift, when combined with the thrust of an engine, empowered them to fly. In other words, to overcome the law of gravity, they had to rely on another law–"the law of the wind." I don't care how much they might have tried or how fast an engine they could design, without the power of the wind they would never have left the ground. **Without the power of the Spirit, neither will we.**

So much of the struggle and disappointment many believers face is because we try to fly in our own strength. We try to be good enough to please God, when what we need to do is surrender to His Spirit and let Him be good in and through us. If, like Paul, you've found yourself frustrated with your inability to do the good that you know you should, then take heart. The law of the Spirit has set you free to live in Him!

Lord, I know what's right because of Your law written on my heart. I also know how often I fail. Forgive me for my sins and for disregarding Your Spirit. According to Your Word, I do not have to remain bound by the law of sin and death. You have given me Your Spirit to empower me to overcome. Help me to trust You and to walk in the Spirit every day!

49

Insight
-11-

THE NATURE OF FRUIT

So I say, walk by the Spirit, and you will not gratify the desires of the flesh. For the flesh desires what is contrary to the Spirit, and the Spirit what is contrary to the flesh. They are in conflict with each other, so that you are not to do whatever you want (Galatians 5:16-17 NIV).

HAVE YOU EVER BEEN IN A REAL CONFLICT? I'M not talking about bickering over preferences. I mean a war! I'm talking about right versus wrong, good versus evil, where compromise isn't an option because it would just be wrong. When Paul talks about the flesh and the Spirit, he is talking about real war: an ongoing, constant battle for the heart and soul of people. There is no compromise when it comes to flesh and Spirit. What's good for one is bad for the other and vice versa. As he spells out the works of the flesh, you begin to get the severity of the picture.

The acts of the flesh are obvious: sexual immorality, impurity, and debauchery; idolatry and witchcraft; hatred, discord, jealousy, fits of rage, selfish ambition, dissensions, factions, and envy; drunkenness, orgies, and the like. I warn you, as I did before, that those who live like this will not inherit the kingdom of God (Galatians 5:19-21 NIV).

Note that last line, "Those who live like this will not inherit the kingdom of God." This war is a matter of eternal life and death. The stakes could not be higher! Sadly, if you look around, you will see this battle rages everywhere. Think about the unexplainable things people think, say, and do and the incredible hurt they inflict on each other. Of course, with the availability of global media, we get hourly reports of the most extreme instances of hate and hurt from all over the world. Honestly, it can make you afraid to watch the news.

What new horrible thing has been done today?
What group is being attacked and who is attacking?
What evil and hurtful behavior is being justified or even celebrated?

It feels like people are losing their minds!

Paul gives us some clarity by simply reminding us that this is what flesh does and always has done. All the things we see that seem so shocking and rampant like rage, hatred, violence, and selfish ambition are all works of the flesh. Take a moment to consider how many people you personally know who have suffered because of the rejection of God's plan for family and sexuality. Yet, the "sanctity" of sexual freedom remains the ultimate pursuit of so many, in spite of the obvious hurt and pain caused to individuals, families, and even entire communities.

It all seems so illogical...

51

...until you remember it has nothing to do with logic.
This is what flesh produces and all it can ever produce.

The frustrating thing for followers of Jesus is that we still have to deal with the flesh. While we are set free in Jesus and filled with His Spirit, there is still this ongoing war. However, the good news is that because of the Spirit we don't have to give in to the acts of the flesh. Look at how Paul describes the work of the Spirit in the life of a believer.

Beautiful Fruit

The fruit of the Spirit manifests the character of Christ in every thought, word, feeling, attitude, and action in our lives...

- Words that are kind, not cruel.
- Actions which are self-controlled, not reckless or wanton.
- Words and actions which express God's love, patience, peace, and care for others.

But the fruit of the Spirit is love, joy, peace, patience, kindness, goodness, faithfulness, gentleness, self-control; against such things there is no law. And those who belong to Christ Jesus have crucified the flesh with its passions and desires. If we live by the Spirit, let us also keep in step with the Spirit (Galatians 5:22-23).

I don't know about you, but that sounds beautiful to me. I want that in my life and in the world around me. Picture with me, for a moment, the litany of horrible news that testifies to the unbridled works of the flesh all around us. Now, imagine a loving Father who wants to pour love, joy, peace, patience, kindness, goodness, faithfulness, gentleness, and self-control like healing oil over mankind. That's God's vision and His gift for His people. That's the work of the Spirit.

Remember, it's called the "fruit of the Spirit," and in that description, we find a powerful key to the Spirit-filled life:

**New life is found in the fruit He produces,
not the effort you exert.**

One of our greatest challenges to walking in grace is that we have been raised to try harder, do better, and pull ourselves up by the bootstraps. This totally misses the idea of "fruit," and I think it is a primary reason so many of us feel so dissatisfied by our spiritual growth and life. I can't manufacture fruit no matter how hard I try. It has to be grown. Most importantly, it's not the fruit of *you* or the fruit of *me*, it's the fruit of **the Spirit**. Only He can produce the love, joy, and peace that we know should be the fruit of our lives. Following His Spirit is what produces the fruit and crucifies the flesh with all its passions and desires. In other words, He is the one who produces the fruit because we cannot.

Thank You, Holy Spirit, for being the source of my new life in Christ. Thank You for filling me with love, joy, peace, patience, kindness, goodness, faithfulness, gentleness, and self-control, which is the very character of Jesus. I pray that Your nature would become the fragrance of my life. Lord, teach me to rest in You daily, and help me to follow You in obedience as You grow Your nature in me.

Insight
-12-

THE HOPE OF HOLINESS

As obedient children, do not be conformed to the passions of your former ignorance, but as he who called you is holy, you also be holy in all your conduct, since it is written, "You shall be holy, for I am holy" (1 Peter 1:14-16).

HOLINESS IS A BEAUTIFUL THING. IT IS THE VERY character and nature of God in which we are invited to walk. But in my experience holiness has gotten a bad rap in much of the church.

I grew up in churches that far too often tried to preach and define holiness by an external list of do's and don'ts. Please understand, I think this came from a real desire to please the Lord by being different from the world around us. There was a serious effort to work hard to be holy because the Bible said we should be holy. The problem was, we naturally drifted to focusing on things we could control—the externals. We could keep score, compare, and even judge the contestants. So naturally, things went downhill from there because all of this totally misses the real point of holiness.

I had a disturbing confrontation with this reality a few years back when a group of men from our church wanted to start and publicize a cigar group, where guys would come to be challenged in their faith journey, and smoke cigars together. As you might expect, we had some people who strongly objected to the idea of the group. These were really sincere people who loved Jesus, but I must admit I was deeply disturbed by the questions that accompanied their objection.

Then what is the difference between us and the world?
How will anyone know that we are different?

Shocked, I asked, "You mean you don't know? Do you really think Jesus said, 'By this will all men know you are my disciples... that you don't have a cigar group, or that you wear this, or you don't taste this, or you don't touch that?'"

Regardless of how you feel about cigar groups, you see the problem. The Gospel is full of ways we are going to be different and they have nothing to do with many of the things that we associate with holiness. Think about things like:

- *The life marked by the fruit of the Spirit.*
- *The way we passionately love Jesus and follow Him no matter what.*
- *The way we truly love one another, which Jesus said would really identify us.*
- *The way we love and care for the poor in practical ways.*
- *The way we love our enemies, even when they are trying to hurt us.*
- *The way we believe the Word of God and walk in obedient faith, no matter the cost.*

If you really want to know what makes us different, this biblical list is a great place to start. It's who we are to be as followers of Jesus. That's what sets us apart. That is what holiness looks like. A heart that is passionately on fire and wholly His.

Take a moment to consider your attitude and approach to holiness.

Have you made holiness an external list of do's and don'ts?

Do you find yourself avoiding the subject out of guilt or frustration?

Or have you simply given up on the idea of being holy?

Peter sums it up in 1 Peter 1:14-16 when he says, "As obedient children, do not be conformed to the passions of your former ignorance, but as he who called you is holy, you also be holy in all your conduct since it is written, 'You shall be holy, for I am holy'."

Holiness is being like Him.

As a young man in the church who really cared about my faith, when I read that passage, I would just become discouraged. I read it as though the Lord was saying, "I was holy, I showed you what it looks like, now you go, discipline yourself, and be holy." There was a part of me that honestly thought, "Well yes, Lord, but you also walked on water and raised the dead, so where does that leave me?" But that's not what He was saying at all.

Years later, as I re-read the above passage in light of the indwelling presence of the Spirit, I realized He wasn't simply giving an impossible challenge but rather offering an incredible provision. What I believe He is saying is, "Be holy for I am holy **and, remember, I am in you.**" In other words, **"You can be holy because I am holy in you."** He is going to be holy for us and through us. He is going to build holiness in us by His Spirit. Instead of you and me mustering it up to the best of our ability, He is going to do it by His Spirit. Our role is to cooperate with the Spirit and to live the Spirit-filled life. Our job is to move from self-effort to submission to the Spirit. We do this by simply listening for His voice and doing what He says. That's what the life of holiness looks like and it changes everything!

I can't be holy on my own, but He can be holy in me.
He can in you, too.

Thank You, Jesus, for the beautiful picture of holiness that Your life gave. Forgive me for the times when I embraced a religious distortion of true holiness. Lord, I long to be more like You! I am so grateful that I do not have to try to be holy in my own ability. Thank You for Your Holy Spirit Who is holy in me.

Insight
-13-

WIND POWER VERSUS WILLPOWER

But I say, walk by the Spirit, and you will not gratify the desires of the flesh (Galatians 5:16).

THE PHRASE "WALK BY THE SPIRIT" IS FAR MORE revolutionary than we might first imagine. It's such a simple, short phrase—it is easy to just rush past it. Yet, this phrase perfectly describes the amazing intersection between the practical reality of living life (or "walking") and the infilling of the Holy Spirit. "Walk by the Spirit" speaks of the power behind my actions. It is a different kind of power which infuses everything I do. It is not my strength or my willpower or my self-discipline. It is walking by the Spirit through a different power working in me.

For many of us, this should be really good news because the truth is, our discipline has failed us, and we know it. It's not that we haven't tried or made commitments and resolutions, it's just that they always fall short. Even the most disciplined among us realize we cannot be good enough, and struggle with times of failure and discouragement. We need another power. We need the power of the Spirit.

That's not to say that discipline or effort has no role in our journey of the Spirit, but it is different than you might imagine. A great picture of the interplay between discipline and the Spirit is the ancient Viking longboat. One of the things that facilitated the rapid Viking expansion near the end of the eighth century was their tactical advantage at sea. The shallow-hulled Viking longboat was faster and could go places other vessels couldn't. Images of the longboat show holes all along the hull for oars so the crew could row when wind wasn't available. However, every good sailor knew that extended rowing was never the objective, sailing was. In a sense, the effort or discipline of rowing was to get them to the power of the wind. The wind is what gave life to the ships and caused them to sail. Rowing just got them in place to catch the wind. In a way, our disciplines are a lot like rowing.

Walking in the Spirit requires knowing the difference between willpower and wind power.

Our efforts and discipline should not be focused on trying to please God on our own or trying to be perfect apart from Him. Willpower isn't enough. Our discipline should be focused on getting us to the wind. That's why, for example, the discipline of meditating on God's Word is so significant. We hear His voice and the Word connects us to the wind of the Spirit. The discipline of prayer connects us to the Spirit and we are empowered in His presence. Even the discipline of Christian community puts us in a place where our spirit is encouraged and strengthened as God moves through His people. Our disciplines should be focused on getting us into the presence of the Lord and letting the Spirit fill us. The Spirit will then lead us in righteousness and give us the power to walk differently.

Take a moment to imagine the power to love, like Jesus did, every day at work. Imagine that customer or co-worker you struggle with and picture Jesus loving them through you. The same love He showed His enemies and the forgiveness He showed to those who were crucifying Him is ours to share in the Spirit. Many of us struggle with impatience (note my use of the word "us"). In the Spirit, we have the power to rest in Him and wait patiently for Him to work on our behalf. Willpower is not enough, we need the power of the Spirit, the *pneuma*, the wind.

John the Baptist gives us an interesting insight when he introduces Jesus in Matthew 3:11 saying, "I baptize you with water for repentance, but He who is coming after me is mightier than I, whose sandals I am not worthy to carry. He will baptize you with the Holy Spirit and fire." When he said, "baptize with fire," many of his Jewish listeners would remember the words of the prophet Malachi.

> *But who can endure the day of his coming? Who can stand when he appears? For he will be like* **a refiner's fire or a launderer's soap.** *He will sit as a refiner and purifier of silver; he will purify the Levites and refine them like gold and silver. Then the* LORD *will have men who will bring offerings in righteousness* (Malachi 3:2-3 NIV; emphasis added).

That fire is the cleansing and purifying work of the Spirit. Jesus wants to set us free from the grip of sin and the flesh and He gives us the Spirit to do just that. We have the Spirit and power of God resident in us, but far too often we try to depend on willpower instead of wind power. The minute we are tempted by sin, we should go immediately to the Spirit and say, "Lord, I need Your strength. Please, empower me. I don't want to give in to this temptation. I don't want to give in to that thought, that impulse, that behavior, that anger, that rage, I don't want to say that thing."

What would happen,
if instead of trying to muscle up the discipline to fight sin,
we went to the Spirit and asked for His power?

Paul gave us the answer in the passage we started with: "But I say, walk by the Spirit, and you will not gratify the desires of the flesh." Hebrews 12:1 invites us to throw off the sin that so easily entangles us. The secret is to raise our sails and surrender to the power of the wind: the Holy Spirit of God living in each one of us!

> *Thank You, Lord, for the power of Your Spirit. You move like the wind and You purify like fire. Forgive me for relying on my own willpower in trying to follow You. Help me to walk in the simple, daily disciplines that connect me to Your Spirit. My heart's desire is to truly walk by the Spirit. Fill my life with Your presence and empower me to follow closely and keep my eyes on You.*

Insight
-14-

LEARNING TO HEAR

But if you are led by the Spirit you are not under the law (Galatians 5:18).

THE PHRASE "WALKING BY THE SPIRIT" SPEAKS TO the Spirit enabling us to walk in a different power—His power. However, the phrase "led by the Spirit" opens up another aspect of the Spirit-filled life. Being led by the Spirit involves learning to recognize and respond to a different voice. Whether you are aware of it or not, every day, each one of us responds to different voices. Stop and think about it...

A parent that you could never quite please whose criticism is still with you,

Ambition or financial fear that has driven you to repeated compromise,

The constant drumbeat of societal pressure or political correctness,

Doubt and insecurity which causes you to second guess every move,

*Or possibly people's opinion of you
and simply wanting to be accepted*

*So many voices...
Which one are you going to follow?*

Being led by the Spirit is choosing to respond to and follow one voice. In the midst of all the noise and the competing opinions, it is getting quiet and learning to discern *the* one voice—His. It is listening for Him and following where He leads.

A very practical way to put this into practice is to start every day with a simple prayer, "Lord, open my ears and my heart to hear You clearly, and empower me to follow where You lead." This is a prayer that God always answers!

In fact, sometimes the simple act of praying can immediately make God's will more obvious. Maybe you've experienced this. The minute you stop scheming, planning, evaluating, or worrying, and start praying, many of those competing voices grow silent as you bring your situation before Him. For example, if you are choosing between being dishonest or telling the truth, just the thought of prayer reminds you that you already know what God will say. That might be an oversimplified example, but you'd be amazed how many times the simple act of bringing something before the Lord makes His direction obvious.

Hearing God's voice is only one part of being led. Once you've heard, you're going to have to follow where He leads. So many people are surprised when God leads in ways that are completely different than what we would ordinarily do. Of course, when we think about it, that is exactly what we should expect. Here's how He said it:

"For my thoughts are not your thoughts, neither are your ways my ways," declares the LORD. "As the heavens are higher than the earth, so are my ways higher than your ways and my thoughts than your thoughts" (Isaiah 55:8-9 NIV).

He is the God of the universe, the Great I Am, the Alpha and the Omega, so don't expect Him to think and react like us. In fact, God will often lead us contrary to our "common" sense, just so it is crystal clear Who is doing what, and Who should get the glory. His desire is that we learn to trust Him more than what we see or understand. That kind of trust only comes through following.

When we were starting River City Community Church, God really put this to the test. Looking back, I can see that He was trying to teach us to hear His voice and put our trust in Him rather than in a system. He did this by leading us to do some very unconventional things which we, and most people around us, didn't understand. For example, He made it clear that we weren't to fundraise like we'd been trained. Not that fundraising was bad, but He was training us that He was our provider as opposed to a donor base or even a congregation. This led to some very difficult years as it impacted our work, our livelihoods, and our families, but it also led to some incredible testimonies because we have truly seen God provide in extraordinary ways! To this day, we don't pass a plate

> ## The Unity of God's Voice
>
> "When God speaks, the test must be that the voice of God always agrees with itself. The spoken word is never out of harmony with the written Word."
>
> -S. D. Gordon [6]

in our congregation and God has met our needs in ways that we'd never imagined possible.

He convicted us of the subtle temptation to use people to meet our needs. As we grew and expanded our leadership team, God challenged us to trust Him with a different approach to personnel. Rather than try to find a person who would fit our needs, we were to take whomever He brought to the ministry, develop them, and help them become who God created them to be. His promise was that He would meet our leadership needs better than we ever could and He has done this many times over.

At times, it felt like our hands were tied. It was almost as though whatever was normal, standard operating procedure for other ministries was off-limits for us. We quickly came to discover that God was simply teaching us to hear and trust Him, rather than just following a training manual. The reason was simple: the most important thing for a follower is being led by the Spirit. He knew we could never accomplish supernatural things with natural techniques. God wasn't teaching us a method; He was establishing a connection to His Spirit.

One word of caution. It is a tragic waste to ask for God's leadership, hear His voice, and then make excuses for why you can't follow. "God, I love hearing Your voice, but I can't do that, I can't go there—people won't understand, they'll think I'm odd or a fanatic." This is where trust comes in. When God speaks, you need to obey! Disregarding God's leading is a dangerous game that can actually lead to the gradual hardening of your heart to the Spirit's voice.

Here are three practical ways to grow in hearing the voice of the Spirit:

Be a person of the Word every day. Learn what He has already said and what His voice sounds like. Get a good Bible reading plan and become a person of the Word.

Be a person who prays. Meet with Him daily to talk about your day, your situation, your problems, and your opportunities. Be sure to leave room for Him to speak and you to listen. He will respond.

Get godly counsel. If you get stuck, seek out a mature believer that you trust, ask them to pray, and get their input on what they hear. You don't have to do this alone, which is one of the great gifts of the Christian community.

The more you listen and follow, the better you will become at discerning the Spirit's voice. He is speaking and leading; the question is, are we listening and following?

Lord, I ask for Your leadership today. Teach me to discern Your voice from all the others. Help me to keep my eyes and ears open to the moving of Your Spirit. Then, give me the courage to follow wherever You lead!

PART THREE:
SPIRIT-FILLED PRAYER

The Holy Spirit as the Spirit of Power helpeth our infirmity in prayer. The Holy Spirit as the Spirit of Life ends our deadness in prayer. The Holy Spirit as the Spirit of Wisdom delivers us from ignorance in this holy art of prayer. The Holy Spirit as the Spirit of Fire delivers us from coldness in prayer. The Holy Spirit as the Spirit of Might comes to our aid in our weakness as we pray.
-Leonard Ravenhill [7]

Likewise the Spirit helps us in our weakness. For we do not know what to pray for as we ought, but the Spirit himself intercedes for us with groanings too deep for words. And he who searches hearts knows what is the mind of the Spirit, because the Spirit intercedes for the saints according to the will of God.
(Romans 8:26-27)

Insight
-15-

THE POWER TO CHANGE THE WORLD

After they prayed, the place where they were
meeting was shaken. And they were all filled with
the Holy Spirit and spoke the word of God boldly
(Acts 4:31 NIV).

ONE OF THE MOST DISTURBING QUESTIONS FACING
the church today is, "Where is the power?" The New Testament
is full of examples of the power of God invading the life and
mission of the church. What happened?

To understand the power of the first church, we should
take a close look at the example of the first followers. They
were so full of the Spirit that they saw the power of God everywhere they went. These first believers quite literally changed
the world.

So, what changed them?

In Acts 1:4-5, we read, "And while staying with them he
ordered them not to depart from Jerusalem, but to wait for
the promise of the Father, which, he said, 'you heard from me;
for John baptized with water, but you will be baptized with the
Holy Spirit not many days from now.'" We know He was talking

about what would happen at Pentecost, but I want us to see how they responded and what they actually did.

Acts 1:14 says, "All these with one accord were devoting themselves to prayer, together with the women and Mary the mother of Jesus, and his brothers."

Acts 2:42-47 is after the infilling of Pentecost and paints a vivid picture of life in the early church. This passage is beautiful because it presents a bit of cause and effect. First, you learn what they did, then you learn what it resulted in.

> **And they devoted themselves to the apostles' teaching and the fellowship, to the breaking of bread and the prayers.** *And awe came upon every soul, and many wonders and signs were being done through the apostles. And all who believed were together and had all things in common. And they were selling their possessions and belongings and distributing the proceeds to all, as any had need. And day by day, attending the temple together and breaking bread in their homes, they received their food with glad and generous hearts, praising God and having favor with all the people.* **And the Lord added to their number day by day those who were being saved** *(emphasis added).*

That passage is so compelling! Something about what they were experiencing was so tangible and real that it was contagious. There was a spiritual dynamic that made people want what they saw. We'll see that the "awe and wonder" was directly related to what they were devoting themselves to.

In Acts 3:1, we're told, "One day, Peter and John were going up to the temple at the time of prayer at three in the afternoon" (NIV). We remember what happens next.

A crippled man asked them for money, but they said, "Well, we don't have any money, but what we have we will give you, in the name of Jesus, get up and walk." In an instant, the man was completely healed.

Luke tells us this simple act of spiritual kindness got them arrested, but upon release, they went back to the gathering of believers to pray again. In Acts 4:31, it says, "After they prayed, the place where they were meeting was shaken and they were all filled with the Holy Spirit and spoke the word of God boldly" (NIV).

Do you see the common thread? We could go on reading through the New Testament and what we would see is that prayer is how they connected with the presence and power of God. In fact, prayer is the central vehicle for the Spirit-filled life. Prayer is how it actually happens.

Prayer is the core behavior of the Spirit-filled life.

Do you want real spiritual power?

Do you want the life the New Testament promises?

Do you refuse to settle and simply go through the motions?

Are you willing to receive a power that will change every part of your life, even the ones that you don't think need changing?

Are you hungry for the full manifestation of the Spirit and the power that the Scripture describes?

The answer is prayer!

I hope you see that we cannot separate these. The Spirit-filled life happens through Spirit-filled prayer. Remember, the life of the Spirit is first and foremost a relational journey with our Heavenly Father. It's sad to realize how many times we try to turn our faith into some sort of contract or task that we're going to carry out with scripture as the manual. That grieves the heart of God and totally misses the point. The essence of our faith is following Jesus as His Spirit speaks and leads us. Prayer is how that happens. We're talking about a vibrant, daily relationship with the Creator who dwells in us.

I'm old enough to remember when the *Star Wars* films first came out. I can't tell you how many well-meaning believers tried to find a Christian theme and make a connection between the Spirit and "the force." The problem is the Spirit is not a force. He's not just some cosmic, impersonal, universal force "out there" somewhere. The Spirit is a person, the very presence of God dwelling in us. Prayer is so critical because it's how we commune with Him.

If we want to be Spirit-filled people who truly experience the power of the Spirit-filled life, it will happen by growing deeper in prayer.

The Spirit-filled life is a life of Spirit-filled prayer.

As you contemplate growing in your prayer life, here are a few questions for you to think about:

How would you honestly assess your prayer life?

What was the last thing you think you heard God say?

What did you do about it?

What is one thing you could do today to go deeper in your communion with the Spirit of God?

> Thank You, Father, that Your Holy Spirit resides in me. Help me to be honest about my weakness in prayer. Forgive me for settling. Also, help me to remember that You are with me and will empower me to follow You daily as You teach me to pray. Remind me to include You in every part of my day as I grow in communion with You.

Insight
-16-

ALWAYS PRAYING

Praying at all times in the Spirit, with all prayer and supplication. To that end, keep alert with all perseverance, making supplication for all the saints (Ephesians 6:18).

EPHESIANS 6:18 IS AN EXTREMELY POWERFUL verse, but one that's easy to overlook because of where it's placed. It comes at the tail end of one of the more visual and well-known passages in all of scripture; the description of the armor of God. The imagery of the armor is compelling: putting on the belt of truth, the helmet of salvation, the breastplate of righteousness, and taking up the shield of faith and the sword of the Spirit. It's a very colorful picture that gives insight into the reality of spiritual warfare.

However, we often forget that verse 18 is a part of the same passage. It describes a critical part of our spiritual armor, but it's almost as though Paul sets aside the metaphors and simply cuts to the chase. Once you are clothed, there is one thing you must do...

Pray at all times in the Spirit!

Paul reminds us that the spiritual world is real, and we are confronted daily with a spiritual war whether we like it or not. Prayer is one of our key weapons. However, while we recognize the importance of prayer to our faith journey, we sometimes don't know how to respond to this verse. He doesn't really mean "at all times," does he? Well, Paul repeats this idea in his first letter to the Thessalonians.

> *Rejoice always,* **pray without ceasing,** *in everything give thanks; for this is the will of God in Christ Jesus for you. Do not quench the Spirit* (1 Thessalonians 5:16-19 NKJV; emphasis added).

Pray at all times,
> *Pray without ceasing,*
>> *Pray continually.*

I struggled with prayer for years. I knew the scriptures about prayer, believed in prayer, and clearly saw the effectiveness of prayer, yet I felt like I wasn't measuring up. As I shared this feeling with others, I found out I'm not alone. In conversations about prayer, when the inevitable question comes up, "how's your prayer life?" most people give the safe and tentative "could be better" response. The truth is, most of us live with varying degrees of guilt because we feel like we should be praying more, and these verses don't help. We look at the idea of praying without ceasing and think, "That's impossible. I have to go to work. How long can I stay on my knees, anyway?" This is how we envision prayer. So, we dismiss these passages, treating them like lofty but impractical ideals.

Pray in the Spirit

"But you, beloved, building yourselves up in your most holy faith and *praying in the Holy Spirit*, keep yourselves in the love of God, waiting for the mercy of our Lord Jesus Christ that leads to eternal life."

-Jude 20-21
(emphasis added)

However, I want to suggest that these verses are *extremely* practical and are, in fact, the key to unlocking a more vibrant prayer life. Consider that the Scriptures encourage us to read and study the Word, but it doesn't say, "read the Word without ceasing." All throughout scripture, we're encouraged to care for the poor, but we're not told to feed and care for the poor without ceasing. No, that distinction is reserved for prayer. Prayer is different because prayer is more than an act or a discipline. Prayer is a constant stream of communication, rooted in how we see our relationship with the Father.

As Christ-followers, we are filled with the living presence of our heavenly Father through His Holy Spirit Who lives in us. He resides in us every moment of every day, which changes everything.

Praying without ceasing is a lifestyle of ongoing communion with the Father through the Holy Spirit. It is learning to engage with the Spirit wherever you are all day long.

Of course, I understand and teach the importance of a specific, daily quiet time of prayer and reading the Word. The gospels tell us that Jesus would often slip away to quiet, secluded places and commune with the Father. He even taught the discipline to pray alone "in secret" with the Father, in your inner room or closet, as a rebuke to those who liked to be seen praying publicly. Daily times set apart for prayer are an important spiritual discipline.

However, we often finish our times of prayer and act like God stays there in our "prayer closet" with our Bible and our notebook. It's almost as if we are subconsciously saying, "God, you stay here, and I'll see you tomorrow. I've got things to take care of and, well, some of it's not pretty. You're so pure, You better stay here in this holy place while I go slug it out in the real world!"

We profess the omnipresence of God and even the indwelling of His Spirit, but forget entirely what it means. Can you imagine if we had any other person with us all day, like we believe God is, and then only spoke to them as often as we speak to God? How rude would that be? Yet, we do it to our heavenly Father every day.

This brings us to the core of praying in the Spirit at all times. God is with us all day, every day. We have the privilege of talking to Him and listening for Him in every life situation. Think about that important meeting, or that difficult conversation, or even that heartbreaking phone call. We have the gift of God's presence with us in all of it. A silent prayer or a quiet pause to listen for His gentle whisper can change everything.

Yes, those quiet times of praying in secret to the Father are important, but we also need to bring prayer out of the closet and learn to pray continually. Then we will see how things change as we face the world through the lens of Spirit-filled prayer.

The Spirit-filled life is a life of Spirit-filled prayer.

Thank You, Father, that I can be in constant fellowship and communion with You through Your Holy Spirit. Help me not to ignore You throughout my day, but to keep Your name constantly on my lips. Teach me to see the world through Your eyes as we walk and talk together.

Insight
-17-

PRAYING IN THE SPIRIT

Praying at all times in the Spirit (Ephesians 6:18a).

I'D LIKE TO START WITH A QUESTION. DO YOU ever feel like prayer is boring or lifeless? Be honest. (Don't worry, God is never thrown or offended by our honest questions.) Take a moment to think about your answer. Now consider this quote from E.M. Bounds:

> **Four things let us ever keep in mind:**
> **God hears prayer,**
> **God heeds prayer,**
> **God answers prayer,**
> **and God delivers by prayer.**
> **-E.M. Bounds** [8]

Honestly, you would think that something so important to our spiritual journey would be more alive and vibrant. Something we are instructed to do "at all times" should be filling and life-giving rather than just another chore. If that's not been your experience, you may be missing one of the key components of the Spirit-filled life, which is Spirit-filled prayer.

If you look at Ephesians 6:18, you'll notice that Spirit-filled prayer is not just praying *to* the Spirit, but praying *in* the Spirit.

That's an interesting and significant distinction. I wonder if this is why prayer can sometimes feel stale or uneventful. Have we unintentionally reduced our prayer life to a one-sided conversation where we pray *to* the Spirit but never really pray *in* the Spirit? I'm not suggesting that we can't speak plainly to God about what's on our hearts, but if that's where our prayers stop, we are missing the best part.

*What does it mean to pray **in** the Spirit versus just praying **to** the Spirit?*

I think one way of approaching this question is to ask it from the opposite direction. From scripture we know that we are both spirit and flesh. What would praying in the flesh look like?

In James 4:2, he addresses this very question. He is talking about how the flesh wants what it wants—right now! *"You desire and do not have, so you murder. You covet and you cannot obtain, so you fight and quarrel. You do not have because you do not ask."* In other words, you cut God out of the equation entirely; if you haven't asked, you haven't really prayed. Then in verse 3, he goes on to say, **"You ask, and you do not receive because you ask wrongly, to spend it on your passions."** What better picture is there of praying in the flesh?

Praying in the flesh is when I make it all about me, which is, of course, exactly what the flesh whines for all day, every day. "It's all about me." Flesh turns our prayers into a wish list: "God, I want. God, I need. God, do for me. I want it, and I want it now!" When I'm praying in the flesh, I've stopped interacting with the Holy Spirit. Instead, I'm treating Him like a genie in a bottle. Sadly, many believers go through life looking for teachings, systems, and formulas to help them manipulate God into doing what they want. This is the essence of praying in the flesh. The end result is, instead of listening for the Spirit, we just let Him listen to us as we tell Him what we want. The great tragedy is we miss the gift of praying in the Spirit.

Praying in the Spirit

In Romans 8:26, the Apostle Paul gives us a beautiful insight into praying in the Spirit. *"The Spirit helps us in our weakness. For we do not know what to pray for as we ought, but the Spirit himself intercedes for us with groanings too deep for words."* Have you ever been watching the news or reading about some devastating situation in the world and just groaned, unsure how to pray? Or it could be something closer to home... a family you know that's falling apart, or a person you care about whose life is being destroyed, and you have to admit, "I don't even know how to pray for that." That's where praying in the Spirit comes in. Paul seems to be stating the obvious when he says we don't always know how to pray.

Thankfully, he continues and introduces the idea that the Spirit intercedes for us on our behalf. The Spirit's groanings intermingle with our own, leading to anointed, Spirit-filled prayer. Verse 27 continues, *"He who searches hearts, knows what is the mind of the Spirit, because the Spirit intercedes for the saints according to the will of God."* What a powerful idea. Him interceding for me according to God's will! Paul is addressing the problem that we don't always know how to pray with the solution that we have the very Spirit of God as our prayer partner.

One of the most beloved promises in all of scripture is verse 28, *"And we know that for those who love God all things work together for good, for those who are called according to his purpose."* However, it's really important to note that verse 28 always comes right after 26-27. We can't separate these ideas. The key to things working out for good, and being called according to His purpose, is the Spirit-filled prayer of verses 26-27, with Him interceding for us according to the Father's will. What an amazing gift!

I want to suggest that one of the reasons prayer can seem so lifeless and lacking is because we treat it as a one-sided monologue instead of truly letting the Spirit begin to pray in, with, and through us. He's more than just a tutor who teaches us how to pray. He is a partner who prays with us. Which brings us to an important question, how do we see prayer?

Do we see it as our list of needs,
or do we see it as a time to engage with the Spirit?

A few practical suggestions as you pray:

Since I don't know how I should pray in each situation,
I'll ask Him and let Him lead.

Since I don't always know what things to pray for,
I'll let Him lead me in making the list.

Simply ask His guidance and write things down
as they come to you.

Pray as He leads.

Learning to pray in the Spirit and letting Him lead us in prayer is the key to transforming our prayer life into something supernatural!

Holy Spirit, I desire to let You lead me in prayer. Change how I approach my times with You. Show me how to get out of the way so You can pray in, with, and through me. Remind me to leave spaces where I listen and You speak. Lord, teach me to pray.

Insight
-18-

PRAYING THE MIND OF CHRIST

*For who has understood the mind of the Lord so
as to instruct him? But we have the mind of Christ*
(1 Corinthians 2:16).

**Spirit-filled prayer moves me beyond praying
for what I want to praying for what God wants.**

FOR TOO MANY YEARS, MY PRAYER LIFE SEEMED
to center on what I wanted God to accomplish; "God, please
bless this situation, heal that friend, please provide this," etc.
Maybe you can relate? Now understand, those aren't bad
prayers, but according to 1 Corinthians 2, they are inevitably
limiting. Notice the Apostle's premise in verses 9-10, *"What no
eye has seen, what no ear has heard, and what no human mind
has conceived—the things God has prepared for those who love
him— these are the things God has revealed to us by His Spirit.
The Spirit searches all things, even the deep things of God"* (NIV).

Consider the vastness of our God and the depths of His
Spirit and will. God has so much more for us than we can
imagine. There is more going on around us than what we see
in the natural. Yet, we generally live, make choices, and even
pray on the surface level of the physical world. God says there
is much more and invites us to go deeper with His Spirit. If you

hunger to know the depths of God, the good news is His Spirit resides in you and wants to teach you and reveal those things to you. Paul goes on...

> *For who knows a person's thoughts except the spirit of the person which is in Him? So also no one comprehends the thoughts of God except the Spirit of God. Now we have received not the spirit of the world, but the Spirit who is from God, that we might understand the things freely given us by God. And we impart this in words not taught by human wisdom but taught by the Spirit, interpreting spiritual truths to those who are spiritual* (1 Corinthians 2:11-13).

The One who fully knows God's heart and mind lives in us. Consequently, we have the ability to pray and live in supernatural alignment with God's will.

It's important to note that verse 14 gives a very important caution. "The natural person does not accept the things of the Spirit of God, for they are folly (or foolishness) to Him. He's not able to understand them because they are spiritually discerned." You should realize that when you begin living and walking in the Spirit, the flesh part of you isn't going to like it or really even understand it. There will be times when you discern the Spirit's leading and find yourself asking, "God, are You sure You want me to do that? Are You kidding me?" And if *you* have questions, you definitely shouldn't expect your family members, your neighbors, or your co-workers, who are not following Jesus, to understand. Don't be hurt or surprised when others don't applaud or approve. It's not just that they don't accept spiritual things, it's that they can't. When you are living the Spirit-filled life you are following a voice which others cannot hear. That's why Paul says the things of the Spirit are foolishness to the carnal mind. The natural person doesn't hear the voice of the Spirit, so they don't understand, and we shouldn't expect them to.

Verses 15-16 are key to understanding how to walk in the Spirit-filled life:

"The spiritual person judges all things, but is himself to be judged by no one. For who has understood the mind of the Lord so as to instruct him? But we have the mind of Christ" (emphasis added).

Stop and consider the gift that this passage lays in our laps. The Word declares that by the Spirit we have the actual mind of Christ. More than anything else, this will radically transform our prayer life. Imagine what could happen as we walk through our days and begin to pray with the mind of Christ instead of just the mind of "me." Rather than simply praying what I want, I begin to pray the thoughts and desires of Jesus. My prayers are infused with a different insight and authority. The next time you see people with problems at work, instead of just saying, "God fix them" or "have them do what I think they should do," ask, "Jesus, what's your heart for them? Give me Your mind as I pray. Show me Your desire and help me to pray according to Your plan."

If you're a parent, imagine praying the mind of Christ for your kids. I think we assume we always know what is best for our children, but what if we don't? We don't know what the future holds, but He does. What if we prayed, "Lord, what is Your desire for my children? Reveal Your heart for their future." Then, as He does, pray according to His will. Those are powerful prayers that change the world!

Praying in the Spirit moves me beyond praying for what I want, to praying for what HE wants.

Lord, thank You for the amazing gift of the mind of Christ. As I pray, teach me to listen for Your mind rather than just speaking mine. I want to see what You see. I want to hear what You hear and then I want to pray accordingly.

Insight
-19-

YOUR PRAYER PARTNER

And this is the confidence that we have toward him, that if we ask anything according to his will he hears us. And if we know that he hears us in whatever we ask, we know that we have the requests that we have asked of him (1 John 5:14-15).

"It doesn't work."

THAT PHRASE SUMS UP THE DISAPPOINTED CON-clusion of many believers after praying and realizing the Lord wasn't going to do what they wanted. Most never voice their disappointment so bluntly, but some have. It's as though they ordered something on Amazon only to discover it wasn't what they thought it was. It doesn't work like they'd hoped. "Is there a warranty? I want to send it back. Prayer doesn't work!"

If you've ever felt that way, the above passage from 1 John 5 should jump off the page at you. When you think about it, these two verses really are a kind of warranty on the effectiveness of prayer. They actually guarantee answered prayer for those who will learn to pray in harmony with the Spirit of God. Through John's letter, the Spirit is giving us a confident assurance in the transformative, life-changing power of prayer.

The Partnership of Prayer

The obvious condition of this kind of confident prayer is praying according to His will. The idea is a partnership where He leads us to pray according to the sovereign and perfect intention of God. Some people see this as minimizing our part in prayer, as though we are simply praying for what God is already going to do. I think this totally misses the greatest work of prayer. When we learn to pray according to His will, we begin an inner transformation. We are molding our will according to His. This is the greatest personal benefit of Spirit-led prayer. Rather than simply treating God like a genie in a bottle, you and I are learning to discern His heart for situations, and to pray in partnership as His children.

**God wants us to go apart and quietly wait upon Him,
until He searches into the depths of our being
and shows us our folly,
our failures and our needs...
-A.B. Simpson** [9]

The Promise of Prayer

When we learn to pray according to His will, He promises to hear and to respond. Stop and consider what is being offered. If I will learn to pray His will versus my will, He promises to give me what I ask. That promise has explosive potential for our prayer life.

Take a moment to think about all the things we already know are God's will for us according to scripture. We can confidently pray for any of those things and know that God will hear and respond.

Praying According to His Will...

- 1 John 5:14-15 promises that God hears and responds when we pray according to His will.
- What are some things that we know are His will according to scripture, and can confidently pray for?

God illustrated this for me powerfully through a need in our ministry. A few years ago, we were looking for a very specific kind of leader to serve on our team. We generally prefer to develop and hire from within; however, we really needed someone who had worked in a larger setting to help us structure for the growth that God was bringing. We were concerned with the cultural fit necessary for a person in this kind of key position. We basically wanted to have our cake and eat it, too. So, we prayed. We applied the 1 John 5 principle of prayer and began to pray what Jesus commanded in Luke 10:2, that the Lord would send workers for the harvest. We felt confident we were praying according to His will.

Within a week or so of praying this prayer, a wonderful couple, who had been a part of our church years before, called me to see what God was doing at River City. They had been transferred from San Antonio to Hawaii and eventually gone into ministry. After serving for over ten years at a great (and very large) church in Hawaii, they were feeling God's call back to the mainland. Since both of them had served as high-level staff members at this church, we ended up hiring them both. We prayed and God brought us not one, but two, incredible, high capacity leaders who were already known and loved by many in our fellowship! All because we made a point to "ask according to His will."

This partnership is what praying in the Spirit is all about. Imagine learning to discern and pray according to God's will in every area of your life. Here are a few practical ways that God has helped me go deeper in prayer as I desire to partner with Him:

Begin with Worship. Worship puts your mind in the place of submission to His Spirit. He is exalted, He is God, and you are not. You're going to learn in another section that worship aligns you with His Lordship. Just focus on exalting Him and Who He is.

Trust the Lord to Lead Your Prayer as You Worship. Simply take note of what comes to mind and pray for that. Trust whatever it is to the Lord. Begin to seek Him in the Spirit, trusting Him to lead. Let Him direct how to pray and what to pray for. No formulas, just listen and follow.

Focus on an Issue You are Facing. Rather than starting with a request, simply meditate on an issue in God's presence. Let Him move your heart. In other words, pray **in** the Spirit instead of just praying **to** the Spirit. Ask Him what His heart is for the situation. As He begins to reveal His heart, pray toward that end. You may find you're praying very differently than you would have because you've discerned the heart of God. The obvious question is, do you trust Him enough to pray this way?

Invite Him to Change Your Heart. When you begin praying in the Spirit, you're going to bump into areas where you discover that your heart is not where God's heart is on an issue. Invite Him to change your heart and to give you His heart. That is a very powerful prayer.

Pray for God's Will to be Revealed and Accomplished. Jesus told us to pray, "Your kingdom come, Your will be done on Earth as it is in Heaven." We can pray this any time and know we are praying with His authority and that He will hear and respond.

You can see how praying in the Spirit is the key to transforming your prayer life from a lifeless, routine exercise into something vibrant, relational, and profound. Try it and see what God does!

The Holy Spirit leads us to pray the very will, the very heart, and the very mind of Christ.

Lead me, Holy Spirit, that I might pray the very will, the very heart, and the very mind of Christ. Your Kingdom come, Your will be done.

PART FOUR:
SPIRIT-FILLED WORSHIP

"It is that the Spirit is the outbreathing of God, His inmost life going forth in a personal form to quicken. When we receive the Holy Spirit, we receive the inmost life of God Himself to dwell in a personal way in us. When we really grasp this thought, it is overwhelming in its solemnity. Just stop and think what it means to have the inmost life of that infinite and eternal Being whom we call God, dwelling in a personal way in you. How solemn and how awful and yet unspeakably glorious life becomes when we realize this."
— **R.A. Torrey** [10]

I appeal to you therefore, brothers, by the mercies of God, to present your bodies as a living sacrifice, holy and acceptable to God, which is your spiritual worship.

(Romans 12:1)

Insight
-20-

SPIRITUAL COMMUNION

"The hour is coming, and is now here, when the true worshipers will worship the Father in Spirit and truth, for the Father is seeking such people to worship him. God is Spirit and those who worship Him must worship in spirit and truth."
— Jesus in John 4:23-24

AS WE TALK ABOUT THE SPIRIT-FILLED LIFE, WE inevitably come to the topic of worship. Worship is one of the truly big ideas of our faith. It is deeply personal as it speaks to our core purpose as created beings. Yet it is also something we engage in congregationally, something we share in the Christian community. Somewhere along the line, the idea of worship became distorted as we used the word "worship" to define the musical portion of our church services. The conversation turned to tradition, style, and preference of music rather than spiritual communion. As a congregational worship leader, I have seen some truly crazy power struggles in the name of "worship."

Early in my ministry, I served on staff at a church which struggled in worship. There was a gentleman who had been a long-time organist. Quite honestly, he was a pretty bad organist, but he was a nice man whose family was well connected and had been instrumental in building the church. His playing was

95

so bad that when told by the music director that a song was in the key of D flat, he said, "Well, I don't know D flat, so I just play in D because it is close." (Musicians everywhere are either laughing or sobbing quietly.) It gets better...

Our music minister had his hands tied because he couldn't get support to gracefully ask this brother to find a ministry that might better suit his gifts. This organ had two large Leslie speakers to cover the sanctuary. One was right behind the organist and the other was across the stage to cover the other side of the room. So, the frustrated music director did the only thing he could do; he turned down the organ speaker right behind the organist and unplugged the other one completely. (I know it's passive-aggressive, but a musician's ears can only take so much!)

The situation became even more ridiculous when an older gentleman in the congregation, who sat near the unplugged speaker, figured out what was happening and began plugging it back in. This cycle went on for several weeks, where nobody said a word, but the music minister would unplug the speaker and the older congregation member would plug it back in!

That same church had a policy that whoever wanted to could just show up and play their instrument without attending any rehearsals. So, at one of our services we ended up with two electric bass players, just sitting next to each other, neither of whom had practiced. It was like dueling foghorns! Suffice to say the music was painfully distracting. Maybe you've experienced church struggles over traditions or preferences in musical style and thought to yourself, "This can't be what worship is really about."

In John, chapter 4, Jesus speaks to the very heart of worship. It began with an unusual conversation with a Samaritan woman. It was unusual because Jews and Samaritans did not associate with one another due to long-standing regional conflicts. The fact that she was a woman, in a highly patriarchal society, made things even more complicated.

You may be familiar with the encounter, which occurred at a well and predictably began with a conversation about water and thirst. But as the conversation went deeper and turned to her lifestyle, she changed the subject by bringing up a longstanding controversy about where to worship. 'You Jews said that the place to worship is the temple in Jerusalem. We Samaritans say we should worship here on the mountain.'

Jesus answered her, saying, *"Woman, believe me, the hour is coming when neither on this mountain nor in Jerusalem will you worship the Father. You worship what you do not know; we worship what we know, for salvation is from the Jews"* (John 4:21-22). Verse 23 is a key verse as we talk about true worship:

> *"The hour is coming, and is now here, when the true worshipers will worship the Father in Spirit and truth, for the Father is seeking such people to worship him"* (John 4:23; emphasis added).

Spirit and truth... I want to suggest that Jesus is giving us much more than just a little phrase to remember. He is giving us the very **nature and purpose of worship**. We'll look more closely at purpose in our next chapter. But what do I mean by saying the nature of worship is Spirit?

The Nature of Worship

I believe Jesus is reminding us that in worship, our spirit is in relationship with His. It is relational, and it is communal, and the connection point is in the Spirit. It's sad and ironic that we focus so much on the externals and have turned worship into something that can be so liturgical, something so formal and programmed, caught up in rote and repetition. The woman at the well was doing exactly what we do, focusing on traditions and externals. "Your tradition is that you worship in Jerusalem at the temple. Our tradition is that we worship on the mountain." How many of us have gotten hung up on our preferences and tradition when it comes to worship?

Jesus is letting us know that we're missing the whole point. Worship isn't about tradition. It isn't about song services, religious activity, styles, or preferences. God is Spirit. Those who worship Him must worship in Spirit!

The very nature of worship is spiritual communion with the Father. I can worship anytime and anywhere. I don't need a pastor or priest. I don't need the band or the organist. I just need a spiritual space to commune with the One Who dwells in me by His Holy Spirit.

Why don't you take a moment right now to just worship Him?

Lord Jesus, I worship You. You are Holy and beautiful beyond description and Your Spirit lives in me. Help me to grow in the simple practice of spiritual communion. Forgive me for getting lost in my traditions and preferences. Thank You for setting me free to simply worship You in the Spirit.

Insight
-21-

THE TRUTH OF WORSHIP

God is Spirit and those who worship Him must
worship in spirit and truth (John 4:24).

IN THE LAST CHAPTER, WE LISTENED IN ON A CON-
versation Jesus had with a Samaritan woman at a well. In an
effort to change the subject from an uncomfortable revelation about her life, the woman brought up a point of division
between Jews and Samaritans over the place of worship. Jesus
dismissed the debate as ultimately missing the point of real
worship. He proclaimed that God is Spirit and that we must
worship Him in Spirit and in truth.

The nature of worship is Spirit, but the purpose is truth.

We understand facts and interact with them all the time,
but truth is more than facts—it is bigger, more encompassing.
Truth is the greater reality of how things are—the order of
things. When we worship in Spirit, we are making a relational
connection with the Father. When we worship in truth, we are
acknowledging, and surrendering to the reality of how things
are. We are putting things back in order.

We live in a world that has tried to tear everything out
of order. We see it every day. Many have simply denied the

Creator's existence and therefore, reject the idea of order altogether. Imagine how the Father must feel to hear His creation arbitrarily declare that killing the unborn is fine because life doesn't really begin at conception. Or that His brilliant design for love and sexuality between a man and wife is simply one option. What must He think as the people He created and loves try to declare that their gender was a mistake and that they can simply pretend to be something other than what He created? These are just a few of the ways that we try to bend reality, God's created order, to fit our desires.

When we try to deny God, deny His presence, deny Him as Creator, and deny His will, it puts our life out of alignment with reality. True worship, which acknowledges our Father for Who He is, is the remedy. Worship aligns us with the truth of Who our God is. It declares and acknowledges His created order and brings our heart, mind, and will back to where it should be.

The Way, the Truth, and the Life

Jesus said in John 14:6, "I'm the way, the truth, and the life, no one comes to the Father but by me." That statement by our Lord is just empirically true. He was not suggesting a topic for debate or asking for our opinions. He was simply stating the nature of how things are—truth. We will either worship Him in alignment with the truth of who He is or find ourselves worshipping a made-up savior. Remember, Jesus also said, "You will know the truth and the truth will set you free" (John 8:32). There is freedom in worshipping Him for Who He really is.

He is the way, the truth, and the life... in us.

The Spirit of Jesus resides in each of us as believers. One of the great gifts of the Spirit-filled life is that His presence in us is a constant reflection of His true character and nature. By His Spirit, the way to Father is always within us. His presence ensures that His truth is our constant companion. Of course, His Spirit is His actual life resident in us, empowering us to follow Him.

> *The Way...*
> *The Truth...*
> *The Life...*
> *The Spirit of Jesus abiding in us.*

Worshipping in Spirit and truth can be as natural as breathing in and out when we are filled with His Spirit.

How we approach worship is truly one of the central issues of our faith. As a pastor and worship leader, I have personally witnessed the transformative effect of worship in people's lives, as pride and resistance give way to love, humility, and surrender in worship. I have seen worship be the turning point that draws individuals into a life of following Jesus. I believe that is because the power of worship is connection and alignment in the Spirit. As we exalt Him in true worship, my spirit fellowships with His Spirit and my life comes into alignment with His truth. This is the joyful communion of worship and what we were created for. Whether privately in the solitude of our hearts or when we gather together, we come into alignment with the beauty and reality of creation and we surrender to our ultimate purpose.

Spirit and truth is more than a catchphrase, it is the secret to going to new places in worship. Beyond the songs, meditations, and prayers, what Jesus is giving us here is a key to unlocking a heart of true worship. Let's make a commitment to leave the debates about songs and styles behind and simply press into His presence. Let's focus on connecting with His Spirit and surrendering to His truth and see if we don't begin to fan the flames of Spirit-filled worship.

The power of Spirit-filled worship is the power of alignment.

Take a moment to worship Him in Spirit and truth.

Just rest in His presence and listen for His gentle whisper.

Begin to exalt Him as Creator and King. Declare the truth of Who He is.

In love, surrender yourself to His word and purpose.

Let your surrendered heart be your song of worship.

Father, thank You that You are here with me... right now. I love You and I seek true communion in the Spirit. Teach me to worship in Spirit and truth and may anything in my life that is out of order be brought back into alignment with Your Lordship, as I live a lifestyle of Spirit-filled worship.

Insight
-22-

THE SPIRIT OF WORSHIP

And do not get drunk with wine, for that
is debauchery, but be filled with the Spirit,
addressing one another in psalms and hymns
and spiritual songs, singing and making melody
to the Lord with your heart, giving thanks
always and for everything to God the Father
in the name of our Lord Jesus Christ, submit-
ting to one another out of reverence for Christ
(Ephesians 5:18-21).

It's not about me.

OUR MOST IMPORTANT TAKEAWAY FROM JESUS'
comments about worship in John chapter 4, is that it's not about
me. Worship is not about me and it's not about you either. It's
about the Father. Period. All the conflicts over worship and the
talk of preferences reveal a serious problem with focus. We're
focusing on *us* when we should be focusing on *Him*.

When we complain about preferring these certain songs
over those other songs, or the way this one leads more than
the way that one leads, we are treating our worship gatherings
like some sort of concert or variety show, put on for our entertainment. We'll decide if we like the show and whether or not

we want to be part of it. In other words, worship is all about "me." Worship is designed to please "me" and make "me" feel good. Of course, this misses the point entirely. What's even more troubling is that this attitude can extend far beyond our corporate worship times to the much deeper issue of how I see my relationship with God overall. Does He exist to please me or do I exist to please Him?

There is a great passage of scripture that gives insight about corporate worship and its power to bring our hearts into proper alignment. It begins with a verse that we hear frequently, but not in this context. This is unfortunate because this is exactly the context in which it is given—the context of Spirit-filled worship.

In Ephesians 5:18, Paul writes, "And do not get drunk with wine, for that is debauchery, but be filled with the Spirit." We tend to focus on the "do not be drunk with wine" part, which is certainly a biblical instruction, but in this context, he is using this as an illustration. As we discussed in a previous chapter, he is talking about being "under the influence." Don't be under the influence of alcohol, but be filled with, or under the influence of, the Holy Spirit! Or, we could use the word control—don't give control of your life over to alcohol, but instead let the Spirit be in control. That's a powerful picture of the infilling of the Spirit.

It is out of this understanding that Paul addresses our times of worship together in community. Listen to his continuation of thought in verse 19: *"Addressing one another in psalms and hymns and spiritual songs, singing and making melody to the Lord with your heart, giving thanks always and for everything to God the Father in the name of our Lord Jesus Christ, submitting to one another out of reverence for Christ."* We worship together, reminding each other of His goodness and faithfulness, which aligns us in reverence of Him and submission to one another. Such is the power of alignment found in Spirit-filled worship.

It is important to note that He paints a picture of worship which is **flowing out of the infilling**. Notice the connection between being under the influence of the Spirit and worshipping together. Worship is a posture of submission and obedience which flows from the Spirit's infilling. The apostle also makes this connection in Philippians 3:3.

For we are the circumcision, who worship by the Spirit of God and glory in Christ Jesus and put no confidence in the flesh (Philippians 3:3).

How do you think we "worship by the Spirit of God?" I imagine it's similar to what we discussed in our section on prayer. The Spirit can empower us and cause us to worship in a way that is in alignment with God's leadership. It's as though He begins to worship through us. This can happen in the Christian community or in our private interactions with the Father. It is simply the Spirit bringing our hearts into the alignment of true worship.

In 1 Corinthians 14:13-14, Paul is again talking about spiritual prayer and worship, but in verse 15 he says, "What am I to do? I will pray with my spirit, but I will pray with my mind also. I will sing praise with my spirit, but I will sing praise with my mind also." In this clear contrast, Paul is pointing out that praying and worshipping with my mind is a wonderful thing. I worship from a place of my understanding of God, His nature, His goodness, and His faithfulness. However, my understanding is naturally limited. When I pray or sing in the Spirit, He is taking me to a different place in prayer and worship. He begins to pray, sing, and worship with and through me. Imagine praying, singing, and worshipping completely under the influence of the Spirit!

*This sheds a whole new light on Jesus' call
to worship in Spirit and truth.*

*I guess the question is, are we willing
to let go of our death grip on control?*

*Are we willing to be led rather than
leading in our approach to worship?*

In a sense, worshipping Him in Spirit and in truth is the defining issue of what it means to be a follower of Jesus.

*Lord, I release control so that I may sing, wor-
ship, and praise You with my mind and with my
spirit. Teach me to truly worship You in Spirit
and in truth.*

Insight
-23-

HEART TO HEART

*"You hypocrites! Well did Isaiah prophesy of you,
when he said: 'This people honors me with their
lips, but their heart is far from me; in vain do
they worship me, teaching as doctrines the com-
mandments of men.'"*–Jesus in Matthew 15:7-9

WE HAVE SEEN THAT THE POWER OF SPIRIT-
filled worship is the power of alignment. True alignment in the
Spirit begins with the heart. It is here we discover one of the
great gifts of Spirit-filled worship.

Spirit-filled worship aligns my heart to His heart.

It has to begin in the heart. The above passage from
Matthew 15 is a sobering warning to any of us who are willing
to look inside and recognize our own potential for "heart drift."
Externally, we continue going through the motions, but inwardly
there is a disconnect. One of the warning signs for a believer is
when we find ourselves going through the motions in worship.
It is discouraging to find that even in times of praise and worship there can exist duplicity between the words of our lips and
the direction of our heart.

As a musician and worship leader, I have been leading and caught myself mid-sentence, because I realized my lips were saying one thing and my heart was focused on another. Things like, "I can't believe the bass player shanked that note again! Why didn't the vocals come in? Oh, that was a nice guitar part." All the while my lips were singing, "It's all about you, Jesus." When this happens, I have to lead my heart in a private moment of repentance and refocusing. Nothing changes on the outside, but everything changes on the inside.

This is actually good practice because I find this kind of thing happens just about every single day of my life. I want to serve and follow Jesus. I tell Him as much every morning, but as I get involved in all the various tasks and responsibilities of the day, I find my heart can drift if I'm not careful. It's times like this I realize the importance of Spirit-filled worship, which aligns my heart to His heart. I never want to be one who "honors Him with my lips, but whose heart is far from Him."

It saddens me to see some people treat the "praise and worship" portion of our service as just a song service or the opening band for the pastor. Those times of corporate worship are times to engage God personally, exalt Him, and bring our hearts into alignment with His. Worship is certainly not restricted to corporate settings when we gather as the church, because worship is simply what we put first in our hearts. However, those important times of corporate worship should train and prepare us for a daily discipline of engaging with the Spirit of God and making sure He is first in our hearts. Proverbs 4:23 warns: *"Keep your heart with all vigilance, for from it flow the springs of life."*

Every time we engage in corporate or personal worship, we have the opportunity to confront three enemies that wage war with our heart.

Distractions, Idols, and Self

Distractions are a constant part of daily life. In fact, as technology has given the whole world access to us every moment of every day through the smartphones in our pockets, the battle with distraction has raged to a new level. I want my heart to be focused on the Father, but I find myself confronted daily by a thousand different distractions. Times of intentional worship help me to quiet my spirit and focus my heart on His abiding presence.

An idol is simply anything that takes the place in my heart that belongs exclusively to Him. We may look at ancient cultures bowing before their primitive idols and think we are far too sophisticated to be caught up in idolatry. Yet, we find ourselves bowing before the altar of our careers, our possessions, maybe a secret sin, or even dancing to the beat of people's opinions of us. Anything that occupies that first place in my heart, which belongs only to Jesus, is an idol. Anything that takes priority over Him or leads me in a direction contrary to His leadership has become a form of idolatry in my life. The only way to deal with an idol is to identify it and root it out of our hearts by the **surrender of worship and the response of obedience**.

Of course, the most incessant rival for first place in my heart is simply me. **Self** is a constant challenge to a heart that desires

Intentional Worship

The very first question of the shorter catechism of the Westminster Confession speaks to the importance of intentional worship. It asks, "What is the chief end of man?" And the marvelous answer is:

"Man's chief end is to glorify God and enjoy Him forever."

to worship Him first. You can call it flesh or the sin nature, but at its core, it is the part of me that wants my way more than God's way. Spirit-filled worship is a regular opportunity to remind myself Who is God and who is not. Every time I bow my heart in worship, I remind myself that **there can only be one seated on the throne of my heart**, and that place belongs to the Spirit of God who dwells in me.

When you begin to engage intentionally in spiritual communion and worship of the Father, you have an opportunity to do some powerful heart work. If God brings something to mind that is vying for His rightful place on your heart's throne, like a relationship, a goal, a dream, or a financial objective, then you are out of alignment. Bring that issue before the Lord in repentance and then engage in a time of Spirit-filled worship. See if other things don't begin to fade in priority as your heart is brought into alignment with His.

The power of Spirit-filled worship is the power of alignment.

Lord, I love You and I pause, right now, to worship You. Be first in my heart. Please reveal anything that would try to compete for that place that belongs only to You. You are my first love. My prayer is that nothing would get in the way of my pursuit of You. As I rest here in Your presence, may my heart be aligned with Yours.

Insight
-24-

LIVING SACRIFICE

I appeal to you therefore, brothers, by the mercies of God, to present your bodies as a living sacrifice, holy and acceptable to God, which is your spiritual worship (Romans 12:1).

LIVING SACRIFICE... I OFTEN HEAR PEOPLE TALK about this passage and I'm not sure we fully grasp what Paul is proposing here. Those of us reading this verse from the comfort of our twenty-first-century framework find ourselves at a serious disadvantage. These few lines might have conjured up very different images for the first-century reader. When we read the word sacrifice, we think of things like going out of our way, giving a little more, doing a little more, and being willing to be inconvenienced for the good of another person or a worthy cause. It's not that those things are bad, they just miss the point.

The first-century audience, Hebrew or not, would have understood the concepts of sacrifice and worship very differently. Anyone familiar with Jewish sacrifices in worship would have two vivid impressions: blood and death. It would be like telling us to present our bodies for the "living slaughter." The sacrifice always died by paying what we call "the ultimate sacrifice." The sacrificial system painted a powerful picture of two foundational and eternal truths. All have sinned (Romans 3:23) and the wages of sin is death (Romans 6:23). These two biblical ideas stand at the center of the sacrificial system. The law also taught that the life is in the blood (Leviticus 17:11), which is why justice demands a blood sacrifice in payment for sin. Simple, brutal, but true.

However, by the time those first readers would have gotten to what Paul wrote in Romans 12, they would have also learned that Christ gave His sinless life to satisfy justice on behalf of all who would put their trust in Him. God demonstrated His love for us by accepting Christ's sacrifice on our behalf even though we were sinners, deserving the death penalty (see Romans 5:8).

So, because of Jesus, I don't have to die, but I am to present myself as a "living sacrifice." In light of the fact that sacrifices always die, this seems like a bit of an oxymoron, doesn't it? Fortunately, in Colossians 3:2-3, Paul sheds some light on this idea: "Set your minds on things above, not on earthly things. For you died, and your life is now hidden with Christ in God."

Our old nature was put to death with Christ and a new nature is alive in Him! This is the Spirit-filled life. Paul goes on in Colossians 3 to list things that were a part of the old life that have no place in this new life. This is what He means by "living sacrifice." In Romans 12:1, Paul is presenting the surrendered life of a living sacrifice as our "spiritual worship." What a profound insight into a heart of worship! The surrender of Spirit-filled worship aligns every part of me with Him. Spirit-filled or "living sacrifice" worship always calls for surrender and obedience in which my daily life is aligned with His life.

I envision three big areas of my existence being brought into alignment with His:

Purpose – My life is not my own. His purposes are central as I plan and dream.

Priorities – My decisions are run through the grid of His priorities, not just my own.

Plans – In obedience, I embrace and execute His plans over my own.

I believe Romans 12:1 is saying that my plans, decisions, and actions all become offerings of worship because they are carried out in surrender to Him. As we have seen, worship is not simply songs, prayers, or meditations. Those might more accurately be called expressions of worship. True worship—"living sacrifice" worship—comes from a heart that puts Him first. Consequently, anything that is done out of a heart of surrender or obedience to the Father becomes an act of worship.

If you're driving along and see someone broken down on the side of the road and the Spirit nudges you to stop and help, even though it will make you late, your decision to stop becomes an act of worship. When God puts the need of a neighbor on your heart and you obey by reaching out, that obedience is an act of worship. When someone offends you and you obey the Spirit's call to love in response instead of reacting in anger, this obedience is an offering of worship. Any act of obedience done out of a heart surrendered to Him becomes the spiritual worship of a living sacrifice.

Every time you respond to the Lord in obedience and say, "Lord, Your way and not my way," you become a living sacrifice offered in worship to Him. Make no mistake, He receives it as such. Your acts of obedience become holy sacrifices of worship because they are reflections of the reality that He is first in your heart and you are His.

This understanding also brings a whole new dimension to our corporate worship gatherings. No longer are we simply passive spectators, singing spiritual songs, or contemplating spiritual ideas. **No, we are the offering of worship!** As we raise our hands in praise, it is as though we are offering ourselves, all that we are, and all that we have, in worship to the Father. This holy surrender is the core of a heart of worship.

My life aligned with His life in Spirit-filled worship.

Lord, I love You and I want my heart and life aligned with Yours. I do surrender myself as a living sacrifice, realizing there are many times when I act more like a sacrifice trying to crawl off the altar. I take this moment to offer all that I am and all that I have to You—heart, soul, mind, and strength. I lift my heart in worship. Let it be Your will, Your way, for Your glory.

Insight
-25-

ALIGNMENT WITH THE THRONE

At once I was in the Spirit, and behold, a throne
stood in heaven, with one seated on the throne
(Revelation 4:2).

THERE IS A THRONE IN HEAVEN. IT IS HIGH, LIFTED
up, and exalted above any other thrones in all of creation. On
this throne sits the one true King of Heaven and Earth. He is
King by right of the simple fact that He is the creator and origi-
nator of all things. He does not take votes or read public opinion
polls. He is the King and Lord over all. Period.

One of the most powerful aspects of Spirit-filled worship is
that it aligns your circumstances with the authority and power
of His eternal throne. No matter what you are facing, worship
brings the reality of His Kingship to bear. You may be facing a
crisis, but the minute you stop panicking and frantically trying
to solve the problem on your own and instead choose to worship, everything changes. The simple declaration, "Father, You
are King, You are the only God, and You are over this situation," brings that situation under the authority and power of
His throne.

Of course, we understand that, empirically, God is King
and Lord over all, regardless of what we or anyone else says.
However, in His wisdom, the Lord has given us free will. We

115

have been given the freedom to choose our course. Far too often we use that free will to take matters out of His hands and into our own. So, while He is King over all, in a very real sense, we insist on being king of our circumstances.

As a pastor, I see this all the time. It breaks my heart to see people I care about refuse the power of the King because they are afraid to trust Him. Instead, they insist on putting their trust in their own resources, their own strength, and the wisdom of the "experts." They have a hard time envisioning the awesome presence and power of the King at work in their situation.

Spirit-filled worship is the key to bringing things back into their proper order. When we truly surrender our will and our responses in worship, it is as though we step off the throne and restore it to its proper owner. Here is the really exciting part...

My circumstances are brought under His authority.
My situation becomes His responsibility.
His power is brought to bear on my issue.
My outcome is in the hands of the King!

A word of practical caution is appropriate here. Surrendering in worship and declaring Him King means I am no longer "king" of my situation. His thoughts and ways are higher than mine. They are different than mine and this creates a unique challenge. He will often lead me against the grain of popular opinion, conventional wisdom, expert advice, and "common sense." If scripture is to be believed, this shouldn't be surprising. He has always done this as a way of making sure we are trusting Him, rather than "leaning on our own understanding" (see Hebrews 11 for a brief refresher course). It doesn't do any good to declare Him King in word, but then refuse Him in deed. However, when we stop trying to rule, start surrendering through worship, and let Him be King, all the power of Heaven is brought to bear on whatever we be may facing. It is as though we and our circumstances are transported into the very throne room of God.

In Revelation 4, the Spirit gives John a vision to share with us. It's as though He pulls back the curtain separating Heaven and Earth and gives us a glimpse of the eternal reality. His language is bold and colorful because He wants us to see, experience, and even feel the majesty of Heaven. Remember, John is simply trying to describe something unlike anything he's ever seen. Words would seem to fail at times like these, but his description is extraordinary:

> *After this I looked, and behold, a door standing open in heaven! And the first voice, which I had heard speaking to me like a trumpet, said, "Come up here, and I will show you what must take place after this." At once I was in the Spirit, and behold, a throne stood in heaven, with one seated on the throne. And he who sat there had the appearance of jasper and carnelian, and around the throne was a rainbow that had the appearance of an emerald. Around the throne were twenty-four thrones, and seated on those thrones were twenty-four elders, clothed in white garments, with golden crowns on their heads. From the throne came flashes of lightning, and rumblings and peals of thunder, and before the throne were burning seven torches of fire, which are the seven spirits of God, and before the throne there was as it were a sea of*

*glass, like crystal. And around the throne, on each side of the throne, are four living creatures, full of eyes in front and behind: the first living creature like a lion, the second living creature like an ox, the third living creature with the face of a man, and the fourth living creature like an eagle in flight. And the four living creatures, each of them with six wings, are full of eyes all around and within, and **day and night they never cease to say, "Holy, holy, holy, is the Lord God Almighty, Who was and is and is to come!"** And whenever the living creatures give glory and honor and thanks to him who is seated on the throne, who lives forever and ever, the twenty-four elders fall down before him who is seated on the throne and worship him who lives forever and ever. They cast their crowns before the throne, saying, "Worthy are you, our Lord and God, to receive glory, honor, and power, for you created all things, and by your will they existed and were created."* (Revelation 4:1-11; emphasis added).

That is the reality of Heaven and Earth and is the true seat of power. Notice how John points out that "day and night they never cease..." This is not someday; this is happening right now! When we bow our hearts in worship, we bring ourselves, our circumstances, and whatever we face into this reality and under the authority of the true King. This is why worship is so central to who we are as Spirit-filled believers. Whether corporately or individually, the theme of worship is always the same:

surrender to the King! Because of that, worship brings us into alignment with the very throne and power of Heaven.

Lord, You are seated on the throne, high and lifted up. You are the only King over heaven and over my heart. I present my life, my circumstances, and everything that I am to You and You alone. Help me to surrender in word and deed. Your kingdom come, Your will be done.

PART FIVE:
SPIRIT-FILLED POWER

It is futile for us to try to serve God without the power of the Holy Spirit. Talent, training, and experience cannot take the place of the power of the Spirit.
-Warren W. Wiersbe [11]

But you will receive power when the Holy Spirit has come upon you, and you will be my witnesses in Jerusalem and in all Judea and Samaria, and to the end of the earth.
(Acts 1:8)

For God gave us a spirit not of fear but of power and love and self-control.
(2 Timothy 1:7)

Insight
-26-

THE POWER OF THE SPIRIT

"Not by might nor by power, but by my Spirit,"
says the Lord Almighty (Zechariah 4:6 NIV).

I LEARNED SOMETHING ABOUT POWER WHILE driving a car... in a parking lot.

We have very large parking lots at River City and so we rent them out from time to time. One of those renters is a group called Dream Cars. They bring a Ferrari and a Maserati into the lot, set up a course, and for $100, you can drive a dream car. Now, I'm not some big car guy and I had no intention of paying $100 to drive a nice car in a parking lot. I couldn't imagine paying that much for three laps around this course, but people were lining up for the chance! I didn't get it.

I think because I'm the Senior Pastor and they wanted to keep renting our lot, they offered me a free spin around the three-lap course. Now that was a price I could live with. So, I went out there with Mike McGuire, our Executive Pastor. These cars were really beautiful and so we took a few selfies like we owned them (yes, we are "those guys").

I chose to drive the Ferrari, got in the driver's seat, and one of the attendants got in with me on the passenger side. It turns out they were not simply going to let me drive off in their

123

$300,000 car. He directed me onto the course, took me to a straight away and told me to "punch it." So, I did.

Wow! No, I really mean it... WOW! I went from 0-60 in like 3 seconds. It was incredible. I'd never felt power like that in a car before. The closest thing to it was taking off in a jet where you have g-force. I'm pretty sure I felt actual g's... in the parking lot! In an instant, I was twelve again and having the time of my life. It was awesome! I'm still not sure I'd pay $100 for three laps, but I can see why people do.

The interesting thing is when I got back to my car something was seriously wrong. I got in, put it in gear, and pressed the accelerator like I always did, but nothing happened... nothing like I'd just experienced. It was broken or at least that's how it seemed. My Toyota, while fun, sporty, and efficient, seemed completely powerless compared to what I had just driven. I had been exposed to real power.

It's one thing to have that happen with a car, but I wonder if that's similar to the perception many people have with their Christian faith. They read about God's power in the Scriptures. They hear about the power from great saints, but it's as though theirs is broken. It's not like what they read at all. They find a significant gap between the promises and what they experience.

The book of Zechariah gives some insight into the source of real power. Zechariah wrote during the rebuilding of the temple, which had been destroyed sixty-six years earlier by the Babylonian invasion in 586 BCE. Some of the people had remained and lived under Babylonian rule in the rubble that had once been their home. Others had been exiled and were now returning, for the first time, to a city which was a shell of its former self. Can you imagine how discouraging a sight this must have been and how impossible the rebuilding must have seemed?

These are the "re-builders" to whom the prophet Zechariah brings God's Word in a series of visions. Chapter 4 gives a specific message for Zerubbabel, the governor of Judah. It is a vision of a solid gold lampstand with a bowl at the top and seven lamps with seven channels to the lamps. Alongside the lampstand are two olive trees with pipes which seem to be providing oil to the lamps.

When the prophet inquires of the Lord what this means, here's what he is told. Read these words carefully:

Proceeding in the Spirit of God...

- Means trusting the promise of God over my own perceptions.
- Requires walking by faith and not by sight.
- Does not focus on the obstacles but rather on the word and power of the Spirit.

So he said to me, "This is the word of the LORD to Zerubbabel: 'Not by might nor by power, but by my Spirit,' says the LORD Almighty. "What are you, mighty mountain? Before Zerubbabel you will become level ground. Then he will bring out the capstone to shouts of 'God bless it! God bless it!'" Then the word of the LORD came to me: "The hands of Zerubbabel have laid the foundation of this temple; his hands will also complete it. Then you will know that the LORD Almighty has sent me to you. "Who dares despise the day of small things, since the seven eyes of the LORD

*that range throughout the earth will rejoice
when they see the chosen capstone in the hand
of Zerubbabel?"* (Zechariah 4:6-10 NIV).

The message is clear: "Not by might nor by power, but by
my Spirit, says the Lord Almighty." I find it significant that this
particular word is addressed first to the leader, Zerubbabel.
Everyone is looking to him, and I can imagine that this task or
assignment seemed hopeless. But God encourages him with
a promise: "Don't despair because you don't think you have
enough power (or money, or manpower, or influence, or whatever); my Spirit is going to provide a different kind of power."
The critical question that he must ask himself is this:

**Do I trust the Lord enough to proceed
with nothing more than the promise of God?**

I guess that's a good question for all of us. Do we have the
kind of faith that will truly depend on God's power rather than
human wisdom or power? I think this is the real issue behind
"powerless faith." We simply don't believe enough to act on
what He says. We confess faith, but when it comes to acting
on that faith, something breaks down. Sadly, we have been so
conditioned to depend on our plans, skills, systems, connec-
tions, and resources that this kind of faith can seem too unre-
alistic... maybe even irresponsible. "I know Your promise, God,
but look at the obstacles... look at how little I have to work with...
I should probably just play it safe."

Of course, there will always be plenty of doubters on hand
to reinforce our fears. But God has a word for the doubters in
verse 10: "Who dares despise the day of small things?" All they

could see was a small foundation in a ruined city. There were certainly some who were old enough to remember the splendor of Solomon's temple before its destruction. They couldn't envision the temple ever being like that again. It seems some were spreading their negative and even scornful doubts to whomever would listen. To the doubters the message was, "How dare you despise what God has determined to do? Take your eyes off the building for a moment and remember Who the Builder really is!"

**Not by might, not by power,
but by My Spirit says the Lord Almighty.**

We get so caught up in what we can or can't do. God's message is clear: It's not about what you can do. The key to experiencing the power of God is actively trusting His Spirit rather than our own limited understanding. Actively trusting means acting on what God is saying rather than what you are seeing.

Where is God inviting you to trust Him today and what are you going to do about it?

Lord, I thank You for the power of Your Spirit empowering me to do everything You have called me to do. Help me to trust what You say more than what I see. Give me the courage to step out in obedience and trust You with the outcome.

Insight
-27-

TALK IS CHEAP

*For the kingdom of God is not a matter of talk
but of power* (1 Corinthians 4:20).

IN 1 CORINTHIANS 4, PAUL HAS TO ADDRESS
critics who are challenging his ministry. He calls them out and
says when he gets there, he'll "find out not the talk of these
arrogant people but their power" (verse 19). Then in verse 20,
he declares, "For the kingdom of God is not a matter of talk
but of power."

There is something about this verse which stirs a longing in
us. In contemporary Christianity, we have to admit, we've got
plenty of talk. In fact, we've taken words to a whole new level.
Between books, sermons, blogs, podcasts, and social media,
we're never in danger of running out of words. But Paul is
talking about something different. He says the Kingdom is not
about talk, but about power.

What comes to mind when you think of the power of the
Spirit? Do you think of particular supernatural gifts, or manifestations, or maybe you envision anointed and convicting mes-
sages? For some of us, the image of prevailing or moving prayer
meetings might come to mind. Any of these unique expressions can cause us to declare, "That was powerful." We would
be right. However, in the last chapter, we looked at a vision

from Zechariah chapter 4, and we heard God make a statement about power. Remember the Lord's words from verse 6:

"Not by might, not by power, but by My Spirit," says the Lord.

I think that vision in Zechariah 4 highlights three very unique traits of the Spirit's power as compared to anything else that we will ever encounter. (You might want to take a moment to revisit Zechariah 4.)

The first trait is simply that the Spirit's power is greater than any other. It is **preeminent.** There is no force on the face of the earth to compare to it. It's not like anything else we encounter. No person possesses this kind of power. It is beyond physical strength, it transcends the power of wealth, personality, or persuasion. It is the eternal, omnipotent power of God. It simply has no equal. No nation, government, economy, or military can stand against the power of the Spirit. He stands alone, transcendent above any other. God was about to do something that seemed impossible. He made it clear that it would not be accomplished by human might or power, but it would be His Spirit at work.

A second interesting observation is that this passage is promising a powerful work of the Spirit to a secular leader for what we might call "regular work." The Spirit's power is **omnipresent.** He wants to empower believers in *every endeavor* and field. I think sometimes we restrict the power of the Spirit to what we consider the "sacred realm," or spiritual work like preaching, prayer, church services, etc. However, Zerubbabel was a governor. He was a regular, governmental leader who was responsible for constructing a building while facing seemingly insurmountable obstacles. Yes, that building was the temple, but the job was actual construction. The Lord promised him, "You're going to see amazing things as you carry out your assignment. This mountain is going to be leveled. You're going to see the hand of God at work."

Being Filled with the Spirit Empowers Me...

- To do what He asks anytime, anyplace, and in any way He desires.
- To see God do amazing things in me, through me, and around me.
- To experience His unending and limitless power.

I think this can be an eye-opener for many Spirit-filled followers of Jesus. The supernatural power of His Spirit is available every day. He wants to move powerfully in your neighborhood. He wants you to trust Him in your work, in your family, and in your finances. The power of God is for every area of our life, not just for the "religious or spiritual" things. Just imagine God leading and empowering you as you seek Him daily in your work or business. Imagine Him doing things that only He can do out in the "real world."

Third, we see that God's Spirit never runs dry. The beauty of His power is that it is **limitless**. Zechariah's entire vision is centered around burning lamps which require oil for fuel. On either side of the lamps are two olive trees with pipes extending from the branches to perpetually provide oil to the lamps (verses 3; 12-14). The oil is representative of the anointing of the Spirit. What a beautiful picture of the Spirit as a constant, never-ending supply to those who will depend on Him. God's power never runs out! It's like what Jesus said to the woman at the well. He told her, "Whoever drinks of the water I give will never thirst again." It's inexhaustible.

I'm reminded of Moses, who was given a glimpse of God's endless supply at a burning bush that never burned up. In South Texas, we have to be very careful when we burn brush because of all the dry cedar, which burns so fast it almost explodes. Moses understood how fire in the desert works and clearly knew how unusual this bush was. Throughout this long conversation, as He listened to God, argued with God, and pointed out how inadequate he was, the bush just kept burning—without being consumed.

It became clear this bush was burning fuel from another place. God was not just telling, but showing, Moses that this mission was not about what he could do. He would have the inexhaustible supply of God's Spirit to empower him to do whatever was needed. Moses just needed to be an obedient vessel and go. The same is true for us.

My prayer is that we do not settle for words or a powerless faith. We live and work around people who need to see the life-transforming power of God. Our churches are hungry for more than words. We are filled with God's Spirit, whose power is **preeminent, omnipresent,** and **limitless!** What if, like Moses, we simply said "yes" and determined to walk in obedience, wherever God leads, trusting Him to provide a power like no other? What might God do?

Thank You, Father, for Your presence in me. Forgive me for doing so much in my own strength when the power of Your Spirit is an inexhaustible supply. Teach me to trust Your power more than my own. Let Your Spirit work in and through me as I say "yes" to Your leading every day. Not by might, nor by power, but by Your Spirit!

Insight
-28-

ARE YOU CRAZY?

The natural person does not accept the things of the Spirit of God, for they are folly to him, and he is not able to understand them because they are spiritually discerned (1 Corinthians 2:14).

I GREW UP IN CHURCHES THAT ACTIVELY SOUGHT the moving and gifting of the Holy Spirit. We knew how to "have church!" (Even though I'm from Chicago, that last phrase should be read with a bit of a southern shout.) We weren't afraid of what are called the "supernatural" gifts. I put that in quotes because I believe they're all supernatural, but you know what I mean.

I'm now going to share something we have all felt or wondered about, but we don't often verbalize. *Sometimes... some* of the people who operated in the supernatural gifts seemed a bit... well... odd. And quite honestly, a few of them were odd. There, I said it—but it's true. It seemed like a disproportionate number of people who operated in what we would call supernatural gifts just seemed a bit out there. Maybe a little awkward or unable to "read the room." As I have thought about this, I have a couple of observations.

First of all, if you are actually moving in the power of the Holy Spirit, you should understand something. It might seem a little odd to people who aren't. Think about it. You are hearing a voice they can't hear, following a direction that they can't see, and doing things that are very different from what they would do. None of this can be called "normal."

Following the Spirit often bypasses things like "common sense" and "conventional wisdom," which are great when you're balancing your checkbook. For things like dental hygiene and car maintenance, you should generally stick with common sense and conventional wisdom. However, following the Spirit is different. When you talk about following the move of God in the life-transforming power of the Spirit, common sense just falls short. Because let's face it, at times like that common sense is just, well... common. And there is nothing common about the power of God! So, don't expect people who are unspiritual to understand what you're doing when you're walking in the power of the Spirit.

As a side note, here's something else I've wondered. Is it possible that some of those who seem a bit odd might actually have an advantage when it comes to following the Spirit's leading? Could it be that those who don't always catch all the social clues might be less distracted with how things appear or what others might think? I'm not sure on this one, but I do know that far too many of us stop short of following the Spirit's leading out of concern over how we will appear to others.

Paul said in the passage above that the natural person cannot understand the things of the Spirit because they are spiritually discerned. We need to accept that the Spirit will cause us to walk in ways that many (ourselves included) may not understand or appreciate. As we consider this, I'd like us to think about three simple words: **see, do, produce**. These three words describe the obvious difference that following the Spirit makes in the life of a believer.

First, the power of the Spirit causes us to **see** things that we can't see in the natural. The Scriptures speak plainly about the spiritual world. It is real and all around us. As the Holy Spirit leads us, we will begin to see a reality that is not visible to the natural person. We see possibilities and pathways others can't really understand. We may discern spiritual warfare or enemies that others don't. As we learn to listen in prayer, we hear the voice and direction of the Spirit where others simply cannot. I think you see where I'm going here. The Spirit-filled believer engages a reality that the natural man or woman cannot. Therefore, we shouldn't be surprised when unbelievers around us don't understand or even write us off as crazy.

Next, as we follow the Spirit, we begin to **do** things that others don't do. In fact, as we follow the Spirit, we do things we wouldn't ordinarily do. Our priorities and values begin to change. We handle relationships, career decisions, financial decisions, and pretty much everything else in a new way. That's because we are following a new leader. Spirit-filled believers routinely come to forks in the road where we must choose between the Spirit's leading and conventional wisdom. The more we follow Him, the more our path will diverge from those who don't. Don't be shaken when friends or family quietly wonder what you are doing. Remember, even Jesus had His family thinking He had lost His mind (Mark 3:21). The Apostle Paul was thought to be insane, driven there by his vast education (Acts 26:24).

Finally, the good news is that as we truly follow the Spirit's leading, we will begin to **produce** a different kind of fruit. As the Spirit works through our submission and obedience, we will begin to see the power of God at work in and around us.

Doors that were closed will begin to open. Hearts that were hard will begin to soften. Mountains will move that can only be attributed to the power of the Spirit at work.

The Spirit-filled life is one of real spiritual power, but it means following paths you wouldn't ordinarily be able to see and doing things you wouldn't ordinarily do. The question becomes, "Are you and I willing to leave the beaten and well-worn path of the natural to take the much less populated way of the Spirit?"

Don't expect the Spirit-filled life to look like a cleaned-up version of your old life. God has much bigger things in store.

Thank You, Father, for Your Spirit in me today. As You show me things I wouldn't ordinarily see, lead me to do what I wouldn't otherwise do, and produce things I could never produce, help me to simply keep my eyes on You. Help me to give grace to those around me who may not under-stand. I pray the fruit of my life would cause others to hunger for more of You.

Insight
-29-

NATURAL VERSUS SPIRITUAL GIFTS

And my speech and my message were not in plausible words of wisdom, but in demonstration of the Spirit and of power, so that your faith might not rest in the wisdom of men but in the power of God (1 Corinthians 2:4).

IF YOU HAVE SPENT ANY TIME IN OR AROUND Christian circles, you know that there are many gifted communicators sharing the truth of the Gospel. One of my favorites is John Ortberg, who has a gifted mind, quick wit, and an impeccable sense of timing. I heard him speak to a group of communicators and I will never forget one thing he shared. He said, "No matter how gifted or talented the communicator, the very best we have to offer, in our own strength, is like crumbs to a starving man. People are hungry for the Bread of Life... they need Jesus." He went on to describe the importance of the Holy Spirit's anointing in our preaching because only the Spirit can bring life transformation. In our own strength we may be able to share "plausible words of wisdom," but that is very different from "the demonstration of the Spirit and of power" described in the passage above.

There is a world of difference between natural gifting and spiritual power. This is what Paul is getting at in 1 Corinthians 2:4. The Apostle was a brilliant and highly educated man. If anyone could have relied on natural strengths or formal training, it was him. But he didn't because he had seen and experienced the power of our resurrected Savior! He knew that what Christ had promised was a radically transformed life that required far more than he or any other person could bring, regardless of their training or talent. I'm afraid we get caught up in what we can do in our own strength and we miss out on what we need: the supernatural power of God. When we face obstacles that seem like immovable mountains, we don't need a class on rock climbing or a coping seminar. We need real power... the power of the Spirit, because He can actually move mountains!

I find it disturbing how often we confuse talent with spiritual gifting. God gives every human being talents and natural abilities, but spiritual gifts are different. They come through the infilling of the Holy Spirit, given only to followers of Jesus. Look at Paul's description in 1 Corinthians 12:4-11.

> There are different kinds of gifts, but the same Spirit distributes them. There are different kinds of service, but the same Lord. There are different kinds of working, but in all of them and in everyone it is the same God at work. Now to each one the manifestation of the Spirit is given for the common good. To one there is given through the Spirit a message of wisdom, to another a message of knowledge by means of the same Spirit, to another faith by the same Spirit, to another gifts of healing by that one Spirit, to another miraculous powers, to another prophecy, to another distinguishing between spirits, to another speaking in different kinds of

tongues, and to still another the interpretation of tongues. All these are the work of one and the same Spirit, and he distributes them to each one, just as he determines (NIV).

Some important points about spiritual gifts:

- Spiritual gifts are given to each one, not just some. Every Christ-follower is gifted.
- The gifts are given to serve the common good, not ourselves.
- Each one's gifts are different, but they come from the same Spirit.
- **The gifts are the Holy Spirit working through us in supernatural ways to do what we could not otherwise do!**

I highlighted that last point because we often act like spiritual gifts are just a new kind of human talent at our disposal and they are not. **The gifts are supernatural ways that the Holy Spirit chooses to work uniquely through each believer.** When I am using my spiritual gifts, He is working through me to produce things I could never produce on my own.

For example, the message of wisdom is not just more human wisdom, but His wisdom which transcends any the world has ever seen. The message of knowledge is the Spirit revealing things you have

Operating in our Spiritual Gifts...

- Takes me beyond my talents and skills.
- Gives me strength and power even when I am weak.
- Releases spiritual power in me to minister His grace to others.

no other way of knowing. Faith, healing, miraculous powers, tongues, and prophecy are all the Spirit uniquely empowering believers to do things they couldn't otherwise do. Add whatever other spiritual gifts listed in scripture, and the same is true—helps, service, administration, leadership, you name it. The gifts are Him going beyond your abilities to do things that only He can do.

This is why it is so important we don't confuse talents with gifts of the Spirit. Talents are about what I can do in my own strength. Consequently, if I'm not careful, my talents can actually get in the way of the Spirit's moving. Our areas of strength and gifting are often where we are most tempted to operate in the flesh. Paul was no exception. When struggling with an area of weakness, he was told: **"My grace is sufficient for you, for my power is made perfect in weakness."** His response was to lean into the reality of his dependence. **"Therefore, I will boast all the more gladly about my weaknesses, so that Christ's power may rest on me"** (2 Corinthians 12:9; emphasis added).

Paul chose God's power over his own strength. I think he knew that talent and strengths are wonderful, but they can't change a person's heart. They will never break the hold of addiction and pride. Human wisdom and resources aren't enough to bring the emotional or physical healing that so many desperately need. No, the desperate need of the world around us requires the transforming work of the Spirit. The good news is He has gifted us to play a part.

Operating in your spiritual gifts simply requires surrendering to the Spirit and letting Him live and move through you. Strengths aren't bad, in fact, they are a different kind of gift, but they are more difficult to surrender. The question is, are you willing to surrender your strength and weakness to let the Spirit do something powerful through you?

Some tips on surrendering...

Listen before you leap – Slow down and let Him speak before you act.

Expect the unconventional – Being Spirit-led generally takes you out of your comfort zone.

Simply speak or do what He puts on your heart.

Let Him work.

Thank You, Father, for giving me spiritual gifts to accomplish Your purposes in the world. Help me to surrender my strengths and weaknesses to You and allow Your Spirit to move through me today.

Insight
-30-

NO EXCEPTIONS

Having gifts that differ according to the grace given to us, let us use them: if prophecy, in proportion to our faith; if service, in our serving; the one who teaches, in his teaching; the one who exhorts, in his exhortation; the one who contributes, in generosity; the one who leads, with zeal; the one who does acts of mercy, with cheerfulness (Romans 12:6–8).

Let us use them...
>   *Not*, let us talk about them...
>   *Not*, let us do another study about them...

THE INSTRUCTION IS CLEAR. LET US USE THEM. Since we have gifts that differ according to the grace given to us, let us use them! You have a unique combination of gifts that the Holy Spirit has invested in you. No one else is gifted exactly like the Lord has gifted you. He wants to work through these gifts to supernaturally advance the Kingdom of God all around you.

There is something in each of us that longs to do something important, significant, something that truly impacts people's lives. That longing is put there by our Heavenly Father, and is accompanied by a unique set of gifts designed to be used to change the world.

Do you know what those gifts are and are you operating in them regularly?

The Spirit's unique gifts in you will affect what you see, how you pray, and where you serve. It's time to stop saying things like, "I don't have much to offer" or "I can't imagine God doing much with me." It's not about what you can or can't do. Remember, He said, "My grace is sufficient for you, My strength is made perfect in weakness." It's *His* grace and *His* strength. It's not about you! Have you ever stopped to think that one of your best qualifications just might be your awareness of your own shortcomings? Might that be the very thing that causes you to cry out for His presence and power?

In an interview for the Global Leadership Summit, Bishop T. D. Jakes gave a powerful exhortation to everyone in attendance. He said, "God has put a seed in each one of us. The question is what are we going to do with that seed? Are we just going to hold on to it and let it remain a seed or are we going to plant it and let it become something amazing?" [12] That is God's intention for what He has invested in you: that by the power of His Spirit it would produce something extraordinary. It reminds me of the passage in John where Jesus says, *"Unless a grain of wheat falls into the earth and dies, it remains alone; but if it dies, it bears much fruit"* (John 12:24).

What are you going to do with what God has planted in you?

Something powerful happens when you operate in the gifts God has invested in you. One of the most exciting things happening these days at River City is how an amazing group of young leaders have started to seriously engage their gifts in ministry leadership. I have to confess; I was a little hesitant when we began considering them for "bigger" ministry positions. A part of me was concerned that they weren't ready and might do some harm to themselves and others if we gave them "too much, too soon." I need to point out right here, I was dead wrong. In fact, the exact opposite was true. As they were given greater responsibilities, they began to grow exponentially! It has been truly awesome to see how God has matured them as they have surrendered their gifts to serve.

I believe the best place to discover and engage your spiritual gifts is within the context of your local Christian community. Gifts certainly shouldn't and won't be restricted to the church, but that is where your journey generally begins. In 1 Corinthians 12, Paul told us that our gifts are for the "common good," referring to the local body of believers. In a healthy fellowship, you can get the opportunity, accountability, guidance, and important feedback necessary to grow in your unique gifting.

If you're not sure where to start, pray and ask the Lord to open your eyes. A great way to begin is by simply meeting a need. It can be something as obvious as a need presented within the body. Step up, say yes, and see what happens. You'll find that serving where you are needed is a great place to start. As you grow, you will begin to sense the Spirit's leading and see needs others don't see. If you find yourself seeing problems or opportunities and thinking, "Someone should do something about that," pay attention to that nudge. Someone probably should do something and that someone may very well be you. That voice might just be the Spirit calling your gifts to action. An important aspect of your unique gifts is that they will cause you to see needs and opportunities others might not see.

Another learning opportunity comes as you observe what God does through your service. Are there kinds of ministry that come more naturally to you? Where do you see the greatest fruit as you serve? The answers to these questions are important because they reveal areas of gifting. If needed, seek appropriate feedback from trusted, mature believers around you. The more you step out in your gifts, the more you will learn about how God created you to serve.

We're supposed to walk and minister in spiritual power, but far too many of us have settled for so much less. In fact, many believers have never even tried. A few chapters ago, I shared the eye-opening experience of feeling the power of a Ferrari and then comparing it to my Toyota. Actually, there was no comparison. After driving a Ferrari, my car felt like a golf cart. I think you'll experience something similar when you begin to surrender to the Spirit's power working through your spiritual gifts. Truthfully, that illustration falls far short when it comes to the things God wants to show you, do through you, and has called you to. His supernatural power, working through you, will bring fruit like you've never seen before!

Lord, thank You for the gifts You have given me! Forgive me for not taking them seriously enough. I invite You to work through me by empowering my spiritual gifts. I'm not going to worry about what other people think or give in to fear. I'm going to start saying yes to the opportunities You bring my way. Open my eyes and give me the courage to follow.

Part Six:
Spirit-Filled Speech

"The book of Acts is the best source that we have to demonstrate what normal church life is supposed to look like when the Holy Spirit is present and working in the church. Here we find a church that has passion for God, is willing to sacrifice—even to the point of martyrdom—and is a miracle-working church. Why would we think that God wants the church to be something different today? Would anyone seriously rather have the church in Calvin's day or the church in twentieth-century America as the model of normal church life?"

-Jack Deere [13]

If I speak in the tongues of men and of angels, but have not love, I am a noisy gong or a clanging cymbal. And if I have prophetic powers, and understand all mysteries and all knowledge, and if I have all faith, so as to remove mountains, but have not love, I am nothing.

(1 Corinthians 13:1-2)

Insight
-31-

LET THE SPIRIT SPEAK

If I speak in the tongues of men and of angels, but have not love, I am a noisy gong or a clanging cymbal (1 Corinthians 13:1).

When I was a child, I spoke like a child, I thought like a child, I reasoned like a child. When I became a man, I gave up childish ways (1 Corinthians 13:11).

WE'RE GOING TO TAKE A look at some sections of scripture that can make people uncomfortable... very uncomfortable. Actually, for many, this topic is just plain scary. Pastors, leaders, and believers in general often avoid these passages because we aren't sure what to do with them. The reason we are unsure is because there has been so much abuse, error, and excess surrounding the gifts we are going to look at.

In 1 Corinthians 13 and 14, Paul unpacks what some have called the

Speaking with Spirit-Filled Speech...

- Begins with the motivation of God's love.
- Communicates the truth of God in love.
- Edifies and builds up the body of Christ.

147

"utterance gifts" of tongues and prophecy. I prefer to think of them as "Spirit-filled speech." I find this description compelling because we live in a world where speech is out of control. We are bombarded with words every day from every direction and the vast majority of them are not helpful or uplifting and are definitely not Spirit-filled. Unfortunately, many in the church have either overly emphasized or completely ignored what the Scripture says about these gifts.

Let's begin right up front by saying clearly: avoiding any truth of scripture because of the abuse of a few is a grave error. That would be like throwing out the entire Christian faith because of the Crusades. The misuse or manipulation of a few in no way invalidates this amazing faith of ours or the power of any section of the Word of God. We cannot skip passages because they make us uncomfortable and these verses are no exception.

It is significant that the apostle sets the table with a rather powerful and convicting admonition regarding love. Some of the most beautiful language in all of scripture is used to describe the selfless nature of real love. Apostle Paul plainly states that even the most heavenly use of tongues is just noise if the words are not uttered in love. Of course, it's not only the gift of tongues or prophecy that must be exercised in love. Great leaps of faith and acts of supreme sacrifice are also included as meaningless apart from a deep motivation of love. What a beautiful declaration of our Father's main priority. As wonderful as gifts and sacrifices may be, love is the very nature of our God and is the key to transforming the human heart. Nothing else comes close.

Notice the phrase Paul uses to turn the discussion to the gifts and particularly Spirit-filled speech: "Pursue love, and earnestly desire the spiritual gifts..." (1 Corinthians 14:1a). This little transition is highly instructive. It's wonderful to desire, even **earnestly** desire spiritual gifts, but we are not to pursue them. Love is the thing we are to pursue. This is a fantastic guideline as we prepare ourselves to be used by God. Desire the gifts but pursue love.

Even a casual reading of 1 Corinthians chapters 12-14 reveals that this was a huge problem with the church in Corinth. It seems like they had developed some kind of "gift hierarchy" based on how public a gift was (or wasn't), and in the process, certain gifts began to be misused. Inevitably, comparison and competition overshadowed the true purpose of all the gifts which is to edify and build up the body. The gifts are God's provision for the whole body and it's important to note that **none of us receives all the gifts**. What this means is, if I want the benefit of all the gifts, I need the other members of the body and I must stay connected to the Christian community. Ironically, gifts which were intended to build community and highlight our need for each other have become a source of division and separation.

Time to grow up!

Another remedy for this division and abuse is simply to grow up. Paul's admonition in chapter 13 is to "give up childish ways." This points to the need for maturity as we use our gifts, particularly Spirit-filled speech. In chapter 14, Paul says it this way, "Brothers, do not be children in your thinking. Be infants in evil, but in your thinking be mature" (1 Corinthians 14:20).

One of the key qualities of maturity is the realization that it's not about me. As a child, it's all about you and your needs. Even as you grow, you're focused on *your* schooling, *your* educational decisions, *your* marriage and career decisions, *your* plans, *your* goals, and *your* dreams. But there is one thing that brings all that to a screeching halt and catapults you to the maturity that says, "It's not about me." That thing is parenthood. Once you become a parent, it is never about you again.

Lauri and I started our ministry together in Southern California. While we were there, we had our first child, our daughter, Lauren. A few months after Lauren was born, after four years in California, we packed up and moved back to Texas where both of our families lived. When we arrived home in a U-Haul with everything we owned after a long two-day drive, both sets of our parents were there to meet us as we pulled into the driveway. They literally ran out, hugged us, took the baby, and went back in the house leaving Lauri and I standing in the driveway. Welcome to a crash course in maturity and "It's not about me."

It's not about me.

This core idea should guide our use of all the gifts, but particularly those which are more visible, and thus, more prone to feed our ego. As we begin to look at what we are calling Spirit-filled speech, we should proceed with a heart of maturity and love that says, "It's not about me." I think there is something powerful that happens when we surrender our heart, our agenda, and yes, our tongue for the Father's purpose.

> *Father God, I earnestly desire every spiritual gift You desire to give. Please take every part of me, including my tongue, to be used for Your glory. Help me catch Your vision and see how my Spirit-filled speech can be a blessing to Your church as well as those all around me.*

Insight
-32-

SPIRITUAL LANGUAGE

For one who speaks in a tongue speaks not to men but to God; for no one understands him, but he utters mysteries in the Spirit (1 Corinthians 14:2).

I DON'T KNOW IF THERE IS A TOPIC OF SCRIPTURE that is more confused and often mishandled than what is called the gift of tongues. Whether by hyper-emphasis, complete avoidance, or the arbitrary declaration of obsolescence, this gift has been distorted and the body of Christ has missed out in the process.

I grew up in a church tradition which saw tongues as the "initial evidence" of being filled with the Spirit. Consequently, every person was taught that they should speak in tongues. This created a fair amount of shame and discouragement among those who didn't "get it," as well as some really questionable, though well-intended, efforts to help them along. I personally observed leaders helping people get the gift of tongues by having them say things like "Hallelujah" or "see my bow tie" over and over, really fast, to kind of loosen up the tongue! A friend of mine insists that he knew someone who was told to repeat "shoulda bought a Honda" until the Spirit fell. That one sounds made up to me, but you get the point.

This whole approach seemed misguided to me. The Bible doesn't call tongues the evidence of being filled; so why should we? If you want to find the evidence or "fruit" of the Spirit's infilling, see Galatians chapter 5. As far as everyone needing to speak in tongues, we have to be careful. Paul listed a group of appointments for ministry in 1 Corinthians 12:28—first apostles, second prophets, third teachers, then miracles, then gifts of healing, helping, administrating, and various kinds of tongues.

Then he says in verses 29-30, "Are all apostles? Are all prophets? Are all teachers? Do all work miracles? Do all possess gifts of healing? Do all speak with tongues? Do all interpret?" **The obvious answer is no.**

I don't mean to be disrespectful nor do I want to enter into a theological debate. I just think we need to be careful not to go beyond what the Word of God says on any subject, including this one. However, I do believe that God gave this gift for a purpose and our best response is to humbly open ourselves to what He says on the subject. So that's what I'd like for us to do. Let's start with a question...

What kind of tongues?

I think some of our confusion comes from our failure to recognize that the Scriptures present different kinds of tongues. In 1 Corinthians 12:28, Paul refers to "various kinds of tongues." For example, in Acts 2 we see believers filled with the Spirit and speaking in human languages that they had never learned, but foreigners heard the message in their own languages. In 1 Corinthians 12 and 14, Paul specifically speaks of a kind of tongues for the edification of the corporate body that must be accompanied by the gift of interpretation of tongues. However, there is a third kind of tongues eluded to in the beginning of 1 Corinthians 14. It appears as though Paul describes a kind of tongues that could be called a private prayer language; something shared only between the believer, the Spirit, and our Father. **It also appears that this gift might be available to every believer!**

> *For one who speaks in a tongue speaks not to men but to God; for no one understands him, but he utters mysteries in the Spirit. On the other hand, the one who prophesies speaks to people for their upbuilding and encouragement and consolation. The one who speaks in a tongue builds up himself, but the one who prophesies builds up the church. Now I want you all to speak in tongues, but even more to prophesy. The one who prophesies is greater than the one who speaks in tongues, unless someone interprets, so that the church may be built up* (1 Corinthians 14:2-5).

A Few Observations:
1. The basic framework of the conversation is the superiority of prophecy over tongues in the public setting (unless accompanied by interpretation) because of its benefit to the entire church.
2. In the process, Paul lists some real benefits to the one who speaks in a tongue:
   • Speaks to God
   • Speaks mysteries
   • Builds himself up
3. Paul clearly distinguishes between tongues for private prayer and tongues for public exhortation, which must be accompanied by interpretation.

4. Paul plainly states that he would like everyone to speak in tongues.

In light of some of the abuse and imbalance that I've seen and experienced, I want to be cautious here. But what if this private prayer language is available and beneficial to every believer? What if God has given a way for the Spirit to pray or intercede on our behalf that goes beyond our capacity to pray on our own? It reminds me of the promise of Romans 8:26-27.

Inviting the Spirit to Pray Through You...

- Takes us beyond what our words can express in prayer.
- Gives the Spirit control of our thoughts, feelings, and words.
- Empowers us to intercede beyond our own knowledge and understanding.

Likewise, the Spirit helps us in our weakness. For we do not know what to pray for as we ought, but the Spirit himself intercedes for us with groanings too deep for words. And he who searches hearts knows what is the mind of the Spirit, because the Spirit intercedes for the saints according to the will of God (Romans 8:26-27).

I am not proposing that this is a specific reference to the gift of tongues, but the similarity is striking. I certainly can relate due to my own limitations when it comes to insight in prayer. What does seem clear is that the Spirit wants to take us beyond what our words can express in prayer. Paul states his own resolve nicely.

> *What am I to do? I will pray with my spirit, but I will pray with my mind also; I will sing praise with my spirit, but I will sing with my mind also* (1 Corinthians 14:15).

A word of encouragement: Don't let rigid, theological interpretations or fear of the unknown keep you from experiencing all God has for you. The idea of praying in an unknown tongue can seem scary or even silly, but just remember, it's not you doing the praying at that point. I encourage you to invite the Spirit to pray through you. When you've expressed all you know to express and seem to have run out of words, just let the Spirit pray. Whether it seems like tongues or simply "groanings too deep for words," know that it is the Spirit praying the mind of the Lord on your behalf. If you're hungry for a deep move of the Spirit in your soul, this seems like a great place to start.

> *Thank You, Father, for the gift of Your Spirit praying through and for me. I pray that my fears and biases would not limit how You want to empower me in prayer. Help me to release my tongue to Your control so that You can pray Your mind and Your will for my life.*

Insight
-33-

WHY TONGUES?

For we all stumble in many ways. And if anyone does not stumble in what he says, he is a perfect man, able also to bridle his whole body (James 3:2).

WHEN I WAS IN JUNIOR HIGH, I INVITED A FRIEND from school to spend the night at my house. It happened to be on a night that we had church, so he went with us. Tim was not a believer and the minister that night gave a powerful message on the gospel and an invitation to receive Christ. I really hoped Tim would respond, but he didn't.

Later that night, he asked some questions about what he'd heard and seen. We talked and I asked him if he'd like to receive Christ as Savior. Much to my delight, he said yes, and I offered to lead him in prayer. As I bowed my head, I heard something strange and sensed something wasn't right. I looked up to see my friend with hands raised and a smirk on his face as he pretended to speak in tongues! He didn't want to receive Christ at all. He was making fun of me and what he'd seen at our Pentecostal Church. Naturally, I punched him, and we just went to bed.

While I was somewhat angry that he made fun of me, I understood. He really highlighted a question that quietly bothered me, "Why tongues?" Of all the gifts God could have given to invite greater intimacy in prayer, why tongues? Why something where, as Paul said, "my mind is unfruitful" (1 Corinthians 14:14)? This puzzled me for many years until I was reading through the book of James and came across his teaching on the challenge of surrendering the tongue.

> For we all stumble in many ways. And if anyone
> does not stumble in what he says, he is a perfect
> man, able also to bridle his whole body. If we put
> bits into the mouths of horses so that they obey
> us, we guide their whole bodies as well. Look
> at the ships also: though they are so large and
> are driven by strong winds, they are guided by a
> very small rudder wherever the will of the pilot
> directs. So also the tongue is a small member,
> yet it boasts of great things. How great a forest
> is set ablaze by such a small fire! And the tongue
> is a fire, a world of unrighteousness. The tongue
> is set among our members, staining the whole
> body, setting on fire the entire course of life, and
> set on fire by hell. For every kind of beast and
> bird, of reptile and sea creature, can be tamed
> and has been tamed by mankind, but no human
> being can tame the tongue. It is a restless evil,
> full of deadly poison (James 3:2-8).

What if the gift of tongues is God's way of teaching greater submission by inviting us to surrender the tongue to the power of His Spirit?

I want to be candid about my own journey here. I became a believer and was filled with the Spirit at a young age. In my own journey of the Spirit, I have experienced the gift of tongues on many occasions and I have prayed in a prayer language. One thing I have often experienced is that while my spirit is very much edified, my mind struggles. Why? I think in some way my mind feels out of control. There are times when I have prayed and it's as though I have run out of words, but there is more in my spirit... more to be prayed. It feels like I'm done, but I'm not done, so I just let the Spirit begin to pray in a language that I don't speak. It is a very powerful experience in the Spirit.

However, many times, my mind kicks in and starts protesting. I think this is what Paul was saying when he says the mind is unfruitful. I think the hardest part is letting the mind rest while the Spirit prays. Honestly, I don't like surrendering my tongue. My mind struggles against it. It's humbling—and maybe that's the point.

Giving up control and being humbled in His presence is good for my spirit, my character, and my discipleship.

So, why tongues?

- *If I can surrender my tongue to the Spirit in prayer, maybe I can surrender my tongue to His control when I am in an argument and becoming angry.*
- *If I can learn to let go and allow the Spirit to pray through me in a language that doesn't make sense to me, maybe I can surrender my body in times of temptation.*

- *If He is, by His Spirit, teaching me to surrender my tongue in a prayer language, maybe I can learn to surrender my pride for the good of the Kingdom.*

What if the gift of tongues is simply God's way of training us to surrender the part of us that is the most difficult to control?

I submit these thoughts for your prayer and consideration. Whatever you may feel about the gift of tongues (or any other gift for that matter), I would challenge you not to dismiss any gift or teaching of scripture because it makes you uncomfortable. If His Word teaches it, then we should seek to understand and surrender ourselves to His purpose, not to explain it away. I have found that my comfort is rarely my friend in my pursuit to become the Spirit-filled believer that He created me to be.

God, today, I surrender my tongue and ask Your Holy Spirit to direct my prayer, my decisions, and my actions for Your glory.

159

Insight
-34-

THE GIFT OF PROPHECY

Now I want you all to speak in tongues, but even more to prophesy. The one who prophesies is greater than the one who speaks in tongues, unless someone interprets, so that the church may be built up (1 Corinthians 14:5).

AS MUCH AS WE STRUGGLE IN UNDERSTANDING and contextualizing the gift of tongues, the gift of prophecy can be even more confusing. Images of Nostradamus come to mind as we envision an ancient seer offering glimpses of the future through cryptic revelations. Or maybe we imagine an angry prophet coming down from the mountain to declare the coming judgment. Either way, these narrow stereotypes have caused many of us to simply ignore or completely reject this biblical spiritual gift. Yet a major theme of 1 Corinthians 14 is Paul challenging believers to embrace prophecy because of how it can build up the Christian community.

Similar to tongues, we need to point out that the Scripture speaks of prophecy and prophets in several different ways. For our purposes here, we are not talking about the Old Testament role of the prophet or the New Testament office of the Prophet. While I think there is the distinct spiritual gift of prophecy through which God enables some to minister to the broader church body, **Paul seems to be suggesting that there might be another aspect of this gift that all believers are invited to explore.**

I'd like to propose that it is this aspect which is addressed in the passage cited at the top of this chapter, 1 Corinthians 14:5. This verse is a brief summary of one of the chapter's primary points. Paul wants believers to exercise the gift of tongues, but even more the gift of prophecy, and he lays out two very practical and somewhat obvious reasons:

1. Prophecy is in a known language and can be understood.
2. That understanding is essential for the body to be built up—which is the point.

Look at what Paul says later in verse 39, "So, my brothers, earnestly desire to prophesy, and do not forbid speaking in tongues." 'Earnestly desire to prophesy' seems like an open invitation to more than just a few of us. But before we go there, I think we should define prophecy in its New Testament context. Peter gives some insight in his epistle.

> Above all, you must realize that no prophecy in Scripture ever came from the prophet's own understanding, or from human initiative. No, those prophets were moved by the Holy Spirit, and they spoke from God (2 Peter 1:20-21 NLT).

In its purest sense, **prophecy is simply being moved by the Holy Spirit to speak what God wants to say.** That's it. No thunderclaps or dramatic organ swells; just saying what God gives you to say. It doesn't have to predict the future (although it could because our Sovereign God can speak to what the future holds). Paul is also in no way suggesting that these words carry the weight of scripture or are binding commands on all believers. Look at 1 Corinthians 14:29, "Let two or three prophets speak, and let the others weigh what is said." Prophecies are to be weighed and considered because those sharing prophecies are neither infallible nor above correction. That should ease some of the pressure we may feel. We're not rewriting scripture here. At its core, I believe prophecy is simply the gift of listening and then sharing what the Spirit says. With that understanding, I think every believer could grow in this kind of Spirit-filled speech.

The Gift of Prophecy...

- Shares what God wants to say.
- Encourages and edifies other believers.
- Builds up the whole Christian community.

One obvious challenge is that before God can speak through us, we have to learn to hear what He wants to say. For most of us, this will require a significant increase in our focus and investment in listening. Even as I write this, I am convicted of how much more God wants to say to and through me, if I'll set aside more time and space to listen for the voice of His Spirit.

I know that some of what I'm saying here will seem a bit "out there" to many who read this, but what if it's not? The Scripture is pretty plain and says what it says; it hasn't changed. What has changed is our interpretation and application. I wonder how many of our theological interpretations are simply a way to accommodate or validate our current experience. Shouldn't our experience be evaluated in light of the Scripture's teaching rather than the other way around? What if the reason we don't experience more of the prophetic word is simply that we don't take the time to listen? The question isn't, "Does God still speak," but rather, "Do we still listen?"

It is not reasonable to ask God to speak through us if we are not willing to sit with Him and listen for what He wants to say. I really do believe this is the key to understanding the prophetic word, but it is also the key to renewed levels of growth, power, and effectiveness in the Spirit-filled life. In fact, if nothing came from this entire book but that we began to listen more fervently and intentionally, then it would be well worth the investment and our lives would never be the same.

> *Lord, I thank You that You want to speak to, and through, me. Help me to open myself more fully to Your Word through an increased commitment to listening. Give me the discipline to slow down, create space, and in that space, teach me to quiet my spirit and hear Your voice.*

Insight
-35-

THE BOLDNESS TO SPEAK

*And when they bring you before the synagogues
and the rulers and the authorities, do not be
anxious about how you should defend yourself
or what you should say, for the Holy Spirit will
teach you in that very hour what you ought to
say* (Luke 12:11-12).

HAVE YOU EVER BEEN IN A SITUATION WHERE YOU
felt that God's Spirit wanted to say something through you? I think
most Spirit-filled believers have at one time or another. In Luke
12:11-12, Jesus told His disciples not to worry about what they
would say if brought before rulers and authorities because the
Spirit would reveal what to say in that hour. Don't you think the
Spirit wants to do the same for us? In the last chapter, we looked
at Paul's encouragement to the believers, in 1 Corinthians 14, to
be open to a personal manifestation or expression of the prophetic word. As I said there, I believe it's okay to demystify this
aspect of prophecy a bit so we can see it in its everyday, every-be-
liever context. We understand that the core of discipleship is to
listen for God's voice and do what He says. Well, Paul is simply
telling us to listen for God's voice and to *say* what He says.

This brings up a very serious question as it pertains to
believers sharing a "word" they believe is from the Lord. Will we

have the courage to speak up if, and when, we feel the Spirit's nudge? We live in a culture that has told us, particularly in areas of faith, to sit down and shut up. How will we respond in a time when more and more Christians are acquiescing to the societal dictate that faith should remain private and quiet? Do we have the courage to humbly and obediently share what God puts on our heart when the time comes, and leave the outcome to Him?

One of our pastors at River City Community Church was recently ministering to a couple whose marriage was in serious trouble due to, among other things, infidelity. The husband, whom we'll call Brad, had been with another woman. While the affair was over, and his wife was willing to work on rebuilding their marriage, Brad, who was deeply repentant, could not envision actually being forgiven. His brokenness and shame clouded any hope that his wife, or the Lord, could truly forgive what he'd done. Even if forgiveness was possible, it would take forever before restoration could occur. To help Brad understand how God saw him, the pastor compared God's love and forgiveness to the love Brad had for his own children. "No matter what they do, you don't stop loving them," the pastor told him. "In an even greater way God still loves and delights in you."

That week Brad went to get a haircut and his usual barber was unavailable. He went ahead and took the next available barber, whom he had never met. A few minutes into the cut, after the usual pleasantries, the barber began to speak, "I don't know you, but I know you and your wife are struggling right now. God wants me to let you know that healing and restoration is not going to take as long as you think. He loves you in the same way you love your own children and His desire is to rebuild and restore." Obviously stunned, Brad told the barber some of what he was going through and how that word was an incredible confirmation from the Lord. The barber simply responded, "Yea, I told my wife this morning that I think God is giving me a word for someone's marriage." In that moment, Brad felt God's love and care. He knew God saw him and cared enough to confirm the truth of His word to him personally. Simply sharing what God has given you to say can have a powerful and profound impact.

Hearing that story, could you envision God sharing a message through you? Even as we think about it, fear releases a flood of questions: What about the risk? What if I'm wrong? What if I don't say it perfectly? Rather than worry about those things, what if you simply said to a person or a group of people, "I feel like the Lord is prompting me to share something with you." Could you do that, without claiming to be infallible or perfect or without implying that you must be obeyed? Because if you understand the prophetic word, it's not about you anyway. It's a word from the Lord to build up His people.

Here are four practical suggestions:

- *Listen and ask God to speak through you.*
- *Speak the truth in love. Ask God to fill you with His love as you share.*
- *Present what the Lord says with humility; you're just the messenger.*
- *Submit what you share for consideration, encouraging the recipient to prayerfully confirm what the Lord prompted you to say.*

Growing up, I had a front-row seat to the effectiveness of this approach. My mother, Ginger Azzaro, operated in this gift regularly. It never ceased to amaze me how she would sense a prompting, walk up to someone, often total strangers, and ask if she could share a word with them. I can't tell you how many times that person would begin to tear up with emotion and ask how she knew. My mother would simply say, "I didn't, but God does, and He loves you."

Those encounters would almost always end with hugs and tears of gratitude. Have you ever stopped to consider how many people need to hear a word from our Father and that He might want to speak through you?

Holy Spirit, I invite You to speak through me as You see fit. Give me boldness and the courage to speak at Your prompting. Let Your Word through me be a life-giving reflection of Your love and may I be used to edify others in Your name. May every word be for Your glory, not mine.

Insight
-36-

One More Thing

But, as it is written, "What no eye has seen, nor ear heard, nor the heart of man imagined, what God has prepared for those who love him"— these things God has revealed to us through the Spirit. For the Spirit searches everything, even the depths of God (1 Corinthians 2:9-10).

MANY PEOPLE TREAT THE THINGS OF THE SPIRIT as inaccessible or strictly reserved for a select few who have a unique capacity or temperament for "the deeper life." This is simply not true. God's greatest gift to mankind is His presence residing in us. The cross stands as a powerful reminder of how far God was willing to go to secure forgiveness and freedom so that we could fellowship with His Spirit, Who would live in us. We were created for a vibrant, daily relationship with our Father Who has filled us with His Spirit.

In other words, you were made for this!

When you feel discouraged and wonder if the Spirit-filled life is possible for you, remember:

You were made to walk in the Spirit!

Your spirit was created with a hunger for the presence of God and your soul only finds true rest in daily fellowship and communion with God's Holy Spirit.

You have been given every faculty to hear and follow the Spirit's leading, every day.

When we started Real Life Ministries and River City Community Church, God made one thing perfectly clear: our primary strategy was to be listening to and following the voice of His Spirit. He actually imposed some hard to understand and seemingly restrictive disciplines on us to make sure we didn't simply adopt one of the many growth strategies presented to us on an almost daily basis. These disciplines forced us to look to Him, listen for Him, and the greatest challenge of all–to wait for Him.

One of the ironic things about that time was that we thought the waiting was simply God's way of disciplining us to refine our character, which was, of course, partly true. What we gradually learned was that He was also teaching us the secret to walking in His Spirit. We felt like Daniel LaRusso in the old "Karate Kid" movie, whose karate teacher, Mr. Miyagi, made him do seemingly senseless manual labor instead of teaching him karate. If you've seen the movie, all I have to say is, "Wax on, wax off," and you know where I'm going with this. When Daniel eventually became impatient and protested, Miyagi showed him that the work had been specifically designed to teach and develop the fundamental movements that he would need to practice the sport. He was not simply being tested. Unbeknownst to him, he was learning, and that's exactly what God was doing with us! In many ways, I think we saw waiting on the Lord as simply a trial to be endured, when in reality it was the secret to the Spirit-filled life!

Hurry up and wait.

Waiting is one of the hardest things for us to do. I speak from personal experience here. I don't like waiting and I'm not very good at it. Most of us are impatient and in a hurry by nature and our technology is only feeding the beast. Amazon has not been my friend when it comes to learning to wait. If I want a book, I order and download it instantly on my Kindle reader. If I want to see a movie, same thing. Most of the things I order are now next day delivery. We are so used to having what we want instantly, waiting just seems unproductive and unnecessary. However, the opposite is true. For those who would learn to walk in the Spirit, waiting is actually essential and critically important.

- Waiting forces us to slow down.
- Waiting reminds us Who is really in control.
- Waiting takes our attention off the task and directs it towards the Lord.
- Waiting creates space for God to work, in His time and His way.
- Waiting makes room for the power of God.

Even youths shall faint and be weary, and young men shall fall exhausted; but they who wait for the Lord shall renew their strength; they shall mount up with wings like eagles; they shall run and not be weary; they shall walk and not faint (Isaiah 40:30-3).

One of the hardest parts of those early days was that people around us didn't understand what God was doing. Truth be told, we didn't understand what God was doing either. There wasn't much activity or fruit, just promises and waiting. The results that people expected and even demanded were hard to see.

However, while we were waiting, God was working.

God brought important people and relationships into our lives that we couldn't have arranged. God provided for our needs in ways that we didn't expect. Three times God miraculously gave us property and facilities that we could never have provided for ourselves. In every instance, our primary position was one of waiting, praying, listening, and going against the grain of conventional thought. It wasn't that we weren't working. We were, but it looked different than what many expected. It wasn't **inactivity**, but rather **directed activity**, which came from intentionally waiting on the Lord.

What about you?

Based on the passage at the top of the chapter, I want you to consider this: no eye has seen, nor ear heard, nor heart imagined, what God has prepared for you. That's right, as one who loves Him and has set your heart on following His Spirit, He has things in store that are beyond anything you have seen, heard, or imagined! Those things are revealed and realized by His Spirit at work in and through you.

The question is, "Are you willing to wait on Him?"

Lord, please teach me to wait on You. Help me to create space to pray and listen. Father, teach me to follow Your lead, rather than running ahead of Your Spirit. I ask You to show me the steps of obedience I need to take today, as well as those things that I should just leave in Your hands. One more thing, Father, free me from my need to hear the applause of people, so I can live to please You alone.

EXPERIENCING THE SPIRIT-FILLED LIFE: ACTION STEPS

WE HAVE COMPILED A MONTH'S WORTH OF BRIEF daily reminders and practical applications for you to practice what you've discovered. The end game is not simply greater knowledge, but rather that you and I would continually grow in our experiences of the Spirit-filled life.

Day 1
Being Born Again in the Spirit

Points to Ponder:
Your new birth in the Spirit begins with a total, radical makeover of your body, soul, and spirit.

For Reflection:
Do you respond differently today than you would have before being born again?

How has the Spirit's infilling changed you?

Action Steps:
Start recording your thoughts, patterns, actions, and habits in a daily journal.

For example, on your way to school, work, or shopping, how did you respond to the person who cut you off in traffic or took your parking space?

Day 2
Being Set Free by the Spirit

Points to Ponder:
When the Spirit sets you free, His truth reveals the lies the world has told you.

The Spirit of truth teaches you right from wrong.

Freedom in the Spirit empowers you, thus freeing you from the need to please people.

For Reflection:
How has your perspective on right and wrong changed since your born-again experience?

Would you have described yourself as a people pleaser before you were born again?

How has that changed?

Actions Steps:
In your journal, make a list of some lies from the world that have been revealed to you by His truth.

Pray that God will open your eyes to truth today.

Day 3
Being Empowered by the Spirit

Points to Ponder:
The Holy Spirit's power gives you strength beyond your own talents, gifts, and abilities.

The Holy Spirit empowers you to see the invisible, hear the incredible, and do the impossible. Where your power stops, His power starts.

With God, all things are possible. His Spirit is in you!

For Reflection:
What is God showing you is possible through His empowering Spirit?

Is there anything that makes you uncomfortable about following the Spirit's leading?

Action Steps:
Record a testimony in your journal of how you have experienced the Spirit's power at work in you.

Invite the Spirit to do something unexpected through you today.

Be prepared to share what God does with those He brings across your path.

Day 4
Being Loving in the Spirit

Points to Ponder:
Remember, we love because God first loved us—
His Spirit conceived Jesus Christ and incarnated
His love in time and space.

His Spirit is love in us!

For Reflection:
When do you find it most difficult to be loving?

Action Steps:
As you walk through your day today, allow His
Spirit of love to fill and overflow your words and
actions at all times, in all situations, and through
all of your relationships.

Begin by praying for the power to walk in His love.

Record in your journal how endeavoring to be
more loving in the Spirit affected your actions
and decisions.

Day 5
Hearing the Voice of the Spirit

Points to Ponder:
Here are three practical ways to grow in hearing the voice of the Spirit:
- Be a person of the Word today and every day.
- Be a person who prays today and every day.
- Get godly counsel as you begin to hear the voice of the Spirit.

For Reflection:
Finish this sentence: The thing I find most difficult about hearing God's voice is...

Action Steps:
Take some time in prayer and the Word, with the particular focus of hearing what the Spirit wants to say to you.

Record in your journal what God revealed to you during your time with Him today.

Day 6
Being Led by the Spirit

Points to Ponder:
Being led by the Spirit is choosing to respond to, and follow, one voice: *His voice.*

For Reflection:
As you listen to, and follow, the Lord's voice, what competing voices need to be silenced?

Action Steps:
A very practical way to put this into practice is to start every day with a simple prayer; "Lord, open my ears and my heart to hear You clearly, and empower me to follow where You lead."

Be ready to do things you might not have otherwise done!

Record in your journal how God answered this prayer as you walked through your day.

Day 7
Learning to Wait on God

Points to Ponder:
Many of us struggle with impatience. Waiting is one of the hardest things for us to do, but it is also a wonderful discipline;
- Waiting forces us to slow down.
- Waiting reminds us Who is really in control.
- Waiting takes our attention off the task and directs it toward the Lord.
- Waiting creates space for God to work, in His time and in His way.
- Waiting makes room for the power of God.

The question is: "Are you willing to wait on Him?"

For Reflection:
What have you learned from "waiting" experiences?

What is something that you are waiting on God for right now?

Action Steps:
Record a time in your journal when you *did not* wait on Him, and how that worked out for you.

Record a time when you *did* wait on Him, and how *that* worked out for you.

Day 8
A Life Marked by the Fruit of the Spirit

Points to Ponder:
The fruit of the Spirit is not about what I can do, but rather about what His presence produces in me.

As we mature and grow, we should see more of the life and character of Christ at work in us.

For Reflection:
Who do you know that displays the fruit of the Spirit in their life and relationships?

What do you see in them that causes you to think of them that way?

Action Steps:
Record in your journal a fruit of the Spirit (from Galatians 5:22-23) that you have seen growing in you over the last few years.

Now record a fruit that you'd like to see growing in you.

Spend some time praying for the fruit of His Spirit to continually grow in you.

Day 9
His Abiding Presence

Points to Ponder:
Because of His abiding presence, you can know what God would have you do, and have the power to do it.

For Reflection:
What is something that God may be leading you to do?

What makes you nervous about taking this step of obedience that God is asking of you?

Action Steps:
In your journal, describe a time you felt God was calling you to step out of your comfort zone to do something for Him.

Now, write down something that you think God would have you do today.

Go do it!

Day 10
Victors, Not Victims

Points to Ponder:
A Spirit-focused life has the power to overcome obstacles, and transforms us from victims into victors.

Victory is found in surrendering ourselves to God's leadership, and letting Him overcome the enemies and obstacles that hinder His work in us.

For Reflection:
What obstacles are you facing that are keeping you from being victorious?

Can you think of a promise of God that could lead you to spiritual victory?

Action Steps:
Read Ephesians 6:12-18.

In your journal, list the various parts of the armor of God, including what is named in verse 18.

Let the Spirit lead you in prayer as you do battle on behalf of your situation.

Day 11
Living Like Jesus

Points to Ponder:
We have the power to live like Jesus because the actual Spirit of Jesus lives in us!

For Reflection:
What does living like Jesus look like for you?

Finish this sentence: If Jesus were in my place, He would...

Action Steps:
As you walk through your day today, try to keep your mind focused on Jesus as much as possible by regularly communicating with His Spirit in you.

As you face decisions, ask Jesus what He would have you do.

Record in your journal how connecting with Jesus before making each decision affected your day.

Day 12
God Speaks by His Spirit through His Word

Points to Ponder:
The Word is a gift of His Spirit. He speaks as we read, and meditate on, the Scriptures.

For Reflection:
What is one scripture that the Spirit brings to mind when you're discouraged?

Action Steps:
In your journal, describe a decision you need to make.

Search the Scriptures to find a promise or instruction that God is giving you to help you make that decision.

Say a prayer of faith based on His Word and record it in your journal, then watch for His answer.

Record that answer when you receive it.

185

Day 13
Freedom in the Spirit

Points to Ponder:
Freedom in the Spirit isn't about doing, saying, or feeling whatever you want. It's about discovering the freedom of walking in the Spirit and yielding yourself to His plan.

For Reflection:
What is most challenging about walking in the Spirit?

What is most exciting?

How has yielding to His Spirit changed your prayers, decisions, and attitude today?

Action Steps:
Record in your journal a time when you felt you were being led by the Spirit.

What specifically were you led to do? How did it turn out?

In your journal, list specific differences between walking in *His* Spirit and walking in *your* "best judgement."

Day 14
The Advantage

Points to Ponder:
Consider this startling statement from Jesus, "Nevertheless, I tell you the truth: it is to your advantage that I go away, for if I do not go away, the Helper will not come to you. But if I go, I will send him to you" (John 16:7).

Jesus made clear that it was advantageous for us that He leave, and the Spirit come.

This should highlight how critical the infilling of the Spirit is!

For Reflection:
How has receiving the gift of His Holy Spirit made a difference in how you approach life?

How would you explain the importance of His amazing gift to another believer?

Who do you know who needs to hear about the importance of this gift?

Action Steps:
Spend some time in prayer thanking the Spirit for His presence and inviting His leadership.

In your journal, write a brief description of how the Spirit-filled life changes the believer.

Day 15
Spirit-Filled Prayer

Points to Ponder:
Prayer is how you connect with the presence and power of God.

In fact, prayer is the central vehicle for the Spirit-filled life. Prayer is how it actually happens.

For Reflection:
So, if prayer is the core behavior of your Spirit-filled life, are you making sure you stay connected to the presence and power of God?

Do you see yourself growing in prayer? If so, how?

Action Steps:
Spend some quiet time in prayer bringing the key elements of your day before the Lord.

Practice listening in prayer.

In your journal, write down what you hear God saying.

Day 16
Pray Without Ceasing

Points to Ponder:
Praying without ceasing is a lifestyle: a communion with the Spirit.

This communion is a constant state of walking in the presence of the Lord.

For Reflection:
Do you ever feel like prayer is boring or lifeless?

What have you learned that can make a difference in your prayer life?

How might praying continually change your spiritual engagement?

Action Steps:
Write 1 Thessalonians 5:17 in your journal. Now post this same scripture–which says "Pray continually"–in multiple places you'll see throughout the day (computer desktop, phone home page, sticky notes in the car, etc.).

Every time you see one of these, talk to the Lord. Include Him in every part of your day.

Day 17
Praying *in* the Spirit

Points to Ponder:
Learning to pray in the Spirit and letting Him lead us in prayer is a significant key to transforming our prayer life into something supernatural!

For Reflection:
*How is praying **in** the Spirit different from how you previously prayed?*

Action Steps:
In your journal, describe the difference between praying *in* the Spirit versus just praying *to* the Spirit.

Spend some time in prayer, but this time let the Spirit lead you in what to pray for and how to pray for each item. As something comes to mind, jot it down and then make notes of how the Spirit leads you to pray.

Write down the results in your journal as God answers your various prayers.

Day 18
The Mind of Christ

Points to Ponder:
"For who has understood the mind of the Lord so as to instruct him? But we have the mind of Christ" (1 Corinthians 2:16).

Praying the mind of Christ moves me beyond praying for what *I* want, to praying for what *He* wants.

For Reflection:
It is so easy to confuse what God wants with what we want. Why do you think that is?

How can you know you are praying for what God wants and not simply what you want?

Action Steps:
In your journal, jot down the difference between how we pray when we are praying our mindset versus the mind of Christ.

Choose a topic for prayer focusing on praying the mind, heart, and values of Jesus.

Make note of how different your prayers are.

Day 19
Partnership of Prayer

Points to Ponder:
In Romans 8, Paul describes how the Spirit prays on our behalf, according to God's will, because we don't know how to pray as we ought.

The idea is that we have a divine prayer partner who leads us to pray according to the sovereign and perfect intention of God.

For Reflection:
What do you find difficult about praying in partnership with the Spirit?

Action Steps:
Rather than simply treating God like a genie in a bottle, learn to discern His heart for situations as you partner with Him in prayer.

Some suggestions as you let Him lead you in prayer:

- Spend time thanking Him for all the blessings in your life.
- Trust the Lord to lead your prayers. Simply take note of what comes to mind, and pray in partnership with Him as His child.
- Begin to seek Him in the Spirit, trusting Him to lead.
- Let Him direct how to pray and what to pray for.
- No formulas; just listen and follow.

Remember to record in your journal what you learn in your time with Him.

Day 20
Transforming Your Prayer Life

Points to Ponder:
"Watch and pray that you may not enter into temptation. The spirit indeed is willing, but the flesh is weak" (Matthew 26:41).

As we continue our journey of Spirit-filled prayer, we discover that praying in the Spirit is the key to transforming prayer from a lifeless, routine exercise into something vibrant, relational, and profound.

For Reflection:
In which areas do you find that the spirit is indeed willing but the flesh is weak?

How are you doing when it comes to prayer?

Action Steps:
Use these steps as a Spirit-filled prayer guide:

- Begin with worship. Worship puts our mind in a place of submission to His Spirit.
- Meditate on an issue you are facing in God's presence. Let Him move your heart.
- Pray *in* the Spirit instead of just praying *to* the Spirit.
- Ask Him what His heart is for the situation.
- Invite Him to change your heart if it is not where God's heart is on the issue.

- Pray for God's will to be revealed and accomplished. Jesus told us to pray, "Your kingdom come, Your will be done, on Earth as it is in Heaven."
- Pray with His authority and He will hear and respond.

Record in your journal what God has revealed to you during your prayer time today.

Day 21
The Spiritual Communion of Worship

Points to Ponder:
The very nature of worship is spiritual communion with the Father.

We all desire to spend time with those we love. Spending time in communion with your heavenly Father shows that you love Him, and desire to be with Him.

For Reflection:
What is something that helps you focus your heart in worship?

What do you feel as you spend time worshipping the Lord?

Action Steps:
Find a quiet place for an extended time of worship.

Meditate on the character and love of God.

Record in your journal a prayer of worship and adoration.

Day 22
Worship Him in Spirit and in Truth

Points to Ponder:
"God is spirit, and those who worship him must worship in spirit and truth" (John 4:24).

Worshipping in spirit speaks to how we engage and connect with the Lord.

Worshipping in truth aligns us to reality as we worship God for Who He truly is.

For Reflection:
He is the way, the truth, and the life... and His Spirit resides in you.

Action Steps:
Worship Him for Who He really is:

- Take a few moments to worship Him in spirit and truth.
- Just rest in His presence and listen for His gentle whisper.
- Begin to exalt Him as Creator and King.
- Declare the truth of Who He really is.
- In love, surrender yourself to His Word and purpose.
- Let your surrendered heart be your song of worship.

Record in your journal the truth revealed to you in your time of worship.

Day 23
Intentional Worship

Points to Ponder:
Spirit-filled worship aligns my heart to His heart.

Sometimes there are things in life that become overwhelming, and we just need to stop and worship, remembering Who is God and who is not.

Times of intentional worship help you to quiet your spirit and focus your heart on His abiding presence.

For Reflection:
In what areas are you tempted to forget that He is King?

What does it look like to worship Him no matter what?

Action Steps:

Think of a few areas where you might need to intentionally worship Him and then jot them down in your journal.

As you worship, declare Him King and Lord over each situation.

Pause at the end of your day to reflect on how intentional worship made a difference in you today.

Day 24
Living Sacrifice

Points to Ponder:

"I appeal to you therefore, brothers, by the mercies of God, to present your bodies as a living sacrifice, holy and acceptable to God, which is your spiritual worship" (Romans 12:1).

Being a living sacrifice involves putting three aspects of your life on the altar in worship to Him:

- Purpose – Will you submit your plans and dreams to His purpose for your life?
- Priorities – Will you run your decisions through the grid of His priorities, not yours?
- Plans – Will you obediently embrace and execute His plans over your own?

For Reflection:

Do you find certain areas more difficult to surrender than others?

If so, which ones?

Where are you tempted to be the sacrifice that crawls off the altar?

Action Steps:

Think through your purpose, priorities, and plans for the upcoming week.

In your journal, prayerfully make note of changes that you think the Spirit of God may want you to make.

Open and close each day by saying, "Lord, Your way and not my way." This simple prayer is a first step in becoming a living sacrifice offered in worship to Him.

Day 25
The Power of the Spirit

Points to Ponder:

The key to experiencing the power of God is actively trusting His Spirit and not your own limited understanding.

Actively trusting means acting on what God is saying as opposed to what you are seeing.

For Reflection:

Has your faith taken you to the place of truly depending on God's power, rather than on human wisdom or human ability?

Action Steps:

Think of a situation that you are navigating where your first instinct, based on what you see, might be very different than the leading of the Spirit.

Clearly define the difference, and ask Him to empower you to trust *Him*, rather than your own understanding.

Record in your journal what God is inviting you to trust Him for. Spend some time praying for His leadership, provision, and power.

Write a testimony of how you have experienced His power in your life and what you have learned of His faithfulness.

Day 26
A Faith of Power

Points to Ponder:
"For the kingdom of God is not a matter of talk but of power" (1 Corinthians 4:20).

One of the most incredible aspects of obedience is how it releases the power of God in every situation.

The supernatural power of His Spirit is available every day in every arena of your life.

God loves people and wants to move powerfully in your neighborhood, your church, your work, and your family.

For Reflection:
Where have you seen the power of God at work?

Action Steps:
Pray for the Spirit to move through you as you engage in your various relational circles.

You live and work around people who need to see the life-transforming power of God. Record the names that came to mind when you read this statement. Pray for each name, and ask God how He might want to use you to encourage them.

Day 27
Spiritual Gifts

Points to Ponder:
Some important points about spiritual gifts:

- Spiritual gifts are given to each one, not just some. Every Christ-follower is gifted.
- The gifts are given to serve the common good, not ourselves.
- Each one's gifts are different, but they come from the same Spirit.
- The gifts are the Holy Spirit working through us in supernatural ways, to do what we could not otherwise do.
- Your unique set of gifts are designed to be used to change the world.

For Reflection:
Bishop T. D. Jakes said, "God has put a seed in each one of us. The question is what are we going to do with that seed? Are we just going to hold on to it and let it remain a seed or are we going to plant it and let it become something amazing?" [14]

Do you know what your gifts are?

Action Steps:
Record in your journal what you are going to do with what God has planted in you.

Remember to make this part of your testimony.

Day 28
Letting the Spirit Speak

Points to Ponder:
Notice the phrase Paul uses to turn the discussion to the gifts, and in particular, to Spirit-filled speech: "Pursue love, and earnestly desire the spiritual gifts..." (1 Corinthians 14:1a).

It's wonderful to earnestly desire spiritual gifts, but we are not to pursue them.

Love is the thing we are to pursue.

For Reflection:
Describe what it means to pursue love in the context of using spiritual gifts.

How will following this fantastic guideline prepare you to be used by God?

Do you know what your spiritual gifts are, and are you using them?

Action Steps:
Record in your journal how God continues to use you to love His people, and empowers you to use your spiritual gifts to help others.

Take a proactive step toward using your spiritual gifts within your Christian community.

Day 29
Praying in the Spirit

Points to Ponder:
"What am I to do? I will pray with my spirit, but I will pray with my mind also; I will sing praise with my spirit, but I will sing with my mind also" (1 Corinthians 14:15).

When you've expressed all you know how to express and seem to have run out of words, just ask the Spirit to pray.

For Reflection:
Have you ever invited the Spirit to pray through you?

Action Steps:
Spend some time in prayer and be open to praying in the Spirit:

- Invite the Spirit to lead you in prayer.
- Begin to pray for the first thing that comes to mind.
- Allow the Spirit to guide you in how to pray.
- If you're not sure, ask Him how you should pray and then do it.

Record in your journal what the Spirit led you to pray for today.

Day 30
Saying What He Says

Points to Ponder:

The gift of prophecy is simply saying what God gives you to say.

We are to *listen* for God's voice, and to *say* what He says.

If nothing comes from this entire book, but that we begin to listen more fervently and intentionally, then it is well worth the investment as our lives will never be the same.

For Reflection:

Do you have the courage to humbly and obediently share what God puts on your heart when the time comes, and leave the outcome to Him?

Have you ever stopped to consider how many people need to hear a word from our Father, and that He might want to speak through you?

Are you ready to listen for God's voice, and to say what He says?

Action Steps:

As you consider sharing what God gives you, here are four practical suggestions:

- Listen, and ask God to speak through you.
- Speak the truth in love. Ask God to fill you with His love as you share.
- Present what the Lord says with humility; you're just the messenger.
- Submit what you share for consideration, encouraging the recipient to prayerfully confirm what the Lord prompted you to say.

Record in your journal what you have learned about listening for God's voice.

Day 31
Continuing on in the Spirit

Points to Ponder:
The Spirit-filled life will be an ongoing adventure as you grow in your understanding and experience of His presence!

When you feel discouraged and wonder if the Spirit-filled life is possible for you, remember:

- You were made to walk in the Spirit!
- Your spirit was created with a hunger for the presence of God, and your soul only finds true rest in daily fellowship and communion with God's Holy Spirit.
- You have been given every faculty to hear and follow the Spirit's leading, every day.

For Reflection:
Who do you know who might help you continue to go deeper in the Spirit-filled life?

Who do you know that you could help to walk the Spirit-filled life?

Action Steps:

Continue what you have begun by setting aside time each day to listen for the voice of the Spirit.

As the Spirit reveals His word to you, write it down in your journal and share it with someone else for accountability.

Do what the Lord says and see what He does!

Share your testimony by letting others know what God does as you walk the Spirit-filled life.

NOTES

1 Moody, Dwight L. *Secret Power: The Secret of Success in Christian Life and Work*. Place of publication not identified: ANEKO Press, 2017.

2 Keefauver, Larry, ed. *Holy Spirit Encounter Bible: Experience the Spirits Presence and Power in Your Life*. Orlando, FL: Creation House, 1997.

3 Finney, Charles G., Richard A. G. Dupuis, and Garth Rosell. *The Memoirs of Charles G. Finney: The Complete Restored Text*. Grand Rapids, MI: Zondervan, 2002.

4 Tozer, A. W. *The Root of the Righteous:* Chicago: Moody Publishers, 2015.

5 Stanley, Charles F. *Walking Wisely: Real Guidance for Life Journey*. Place of publication not identified: Thomas Nelson Inc., 2006.

6 Gordon, S. D. *Quiet Talks on Power*. London, 1904.

7 Ravenhill, Leonard. *Wisdom from Rick Joyner*. Shippensburg, PA: Destiny Image Publishers, Inc., 2010.

8 Bounds, E. M. *Prayer and Praying Men*. Place of publication not identified: Wilder Publications, 2018.

9 Simpson, A. B. *The Holy Spirit, or, Power from on High an Unfolding of the Doctrine of the Holy Spirit in the Old and New Testaments*. Harrisburg, PA: Christian Publications, 1895.

10 Torrey, R. A. *The Person & Work of the Holy Spirit*. New York: Cosimo Classics, 2007.

11 Wiersbe, Warren W. *Pause for Power: A Year in the Word*. Colorado Springs, CO: Chariot Victor Pub., 1998.

12 Jakes, Bishop T.D. "God Put a Seed in You." Global Leadership Network, October 9, 2017. https://globalleadership.org/videos/leading-yourself/god-put-a-seed-in-you.

13 Deere, Jack. *Surprised by the Power of the Spirit*. Eastbourne: Kingsway Publications, 2006.

14 Jakes, Ibid.

ABOUT THE AUTHOR

SEAN AZZARO IS THE FOUNDING pastor of River City Community Church, a unique and innovative church in Selma, Texas, a suburb of San Antonio. He and his wife, Lauri, began River City in their home with four other families and have seen it grow into an amazing, vibrant Christian community, as well as a network of churches called the Real Life Network. Sean has also founded Reaching for Real Life, a communication and leadership ministry dedicated to "More people living Real Life by passionately following Jesus."

Singer, songwriter, author, and pastor, Sean has an unusual gift for helping people see spiritual truth through fresh lenses. His rare blend of humor, biblical insight, and real-life truth has helped thousands of people take their next step on the journey to Real Life.

Sean is featured daily on the Reaching for Real Life radio program and podcast. He says of himself, "I am a husband, dad, grandfather, pastor, and musician—who loves his Savior, his family, his job, and going without socks. The best part is, I get to pastor the amazing people of River City Community Church, which really is a church for Real Life!"

Sean and Lauri have 2 married children, 4 grandchildren, and live in the Texas Hill Country.

You can connect with Sean Azzaro at reachingforreallife.org.